THE SHADOW RULERS

Ken Hudnall
Omega Press
El Paso, TX 79912

THE SHADOW RULERS
COPYRIGHT © 2014 KEN HUDNALL

All rights reserved. No part of this book may be reproduced or transmitted in any form or by any means, graphic, electronic, or mechanical, including photocopying, recording, taping or by any information storage or retrieval system, without the permission in writing from the publisher.

OMEGA PRESS

An imprint of Omega Communications Group, Inc.

For information contact:

Omega Press

5823 N. Mesa, #839

El Paso, Texas 79912

Or http://www.kenhudnall.com

FIRST EDITION

Printed in the United States of America

OTHER WORKS BY THE SAME AUTHOR FROM OMEGA PRESS

MANHATTAN CONSPIRACY SERIES
Blood on the Apple
Capitol Crimes
Angel of Death

THE OCCULT CONNECTION
UFOs, Secret Societies and Ancient Gods
The Hidden Race
Flying Saucers
UFOs and the Supernatural
UFOs and Secret Societies
UFOs and Ancient Gods
Evidence of Alien Contact
Intervention
Secrets of Dulce

DARKNESS
When Darkness Falls
Fear The Darkness

SPIRITS OF THE BORDER
(with Connie Wang)
The History and Mystery of El Paso Del Norte
The History and Mystery of Fort Bliss, Texas

(with Sharon Hudnall)
The History and Mystery of the Rio Grande
The history and Mystery of New Mexico
The History and Mystery of the Lone Star State
The History and Mystery of Arizona
The History and Mystery of Tombstone, AZ
The History and Mystery of Colorado
Echoes of the Past

El Paso: A City of Secrets
Tales From The Nightshift
The History and Mystery of Sin City
The History and Mystery of Concordia
Military Ghosts
Restless Spirits
School Spirits

THE ESTATE SALE MURDERS
Dead Man's Diary

Northwood Conspiracy

No Safe Haven; Homeland Insecurity

Where No Car Has Gone Before

Seventy Years and No Losses:
The History of the Sun Bowl

How Not To Get Published

Vampires, Werewolves and Things
That Go Bump In The Night

Even Paranoids Have Enemies

Criminal Law for Laymen

Understanding Business Law

Language of the Law

PUBLISHED BY PAJA BOOKS
The Occult Connection: Unidentified Flying Objects

DEDICATION

As with all of my books, I could not have completed this book if not for my lovely wife, Sharon.

Contents

WHAT'S IN THE SHADOWS?	9
MY THEORY	23
THE ETERNAL CONSPIRACY	65
THE UNSEEN MASTERS	71
WE HAVE MET THE ENEMY AND HE IS US	91
THE OCCULT PATH	111
SETTING THE STAGE	129
THE PLAYERS	161
THE ROCKEFELLER DYNASTY	191
THE GAMES BANKERS PLAY	201
THE PLAN CONTINUES	217
A TRAGIC MEDICAL COVER-UP	237
AND SO?	255

INDEX   **259**

CHAPTER ONE

WHAT'S IN THE SHADOWS?

"Treason doth never prosper, what's the reason? For if it prosper, **NONE DARE CALL IT TREASON.***"*
Sir John Harrington   (1561-1612)

When I wrote the first book in this series, I had the germ of a theory, but knew that it still needed a lot of work. As I delved deeper into the material that I was researching, I soon discovered a very important fact. There exists deeply with the shadows a group of entities who are in fact our rulers. They can't be seen, but they can be discovered through watching the actions they direct in the real world.

At first my theory revolved solely around the mystery of the Unidentified Flying Objects that so many people seemed to be seeing in our night skies. Since, at the time I began the research for my first book, I was doing a nightly radio show I was inundated with data regarding these mysterious lights in the sky. At my invitation, anyone with a

UFO related story could call and be put on the air. This put me in a unique position to be able to get a fairly good picture of what was happening in the so-called "fringe areas" such as UFO landing and similar events.

As I gathered the (almost daily) reports that dealt with these strange objects, I also began to hear about an area of this mystery that I had heard little about, that of human abductions. I began to wonder was this a way for the rulers in the shadows to have direct contact with certain humans?

As a result of interviewing several of the more famous abductees, I began to see that there was much more to the story than what the average person knew about and maybe within the mass of material were a few answers or at least a few clues as to what the answers should be. Upon making this discovery, I began to delve deeper into the strange stories told by the abductees.

ABDUCTEE STORIES

The abductee stories reported to me covered the gamut of the UFO field from "missing time" to medical exams on board "space ships" to classic Men-In-Black encounters. As I collected these stories for my book, I began to see a most unusual pattern. In my younger days I read a lot of books regarding myths and legends form other countries.

To my surprise, I found that, in many cases, some of the details reported by the modern abductees had a striking similarity to stories told by people who had allegedly been abducted by fairies and other such, so-called, fictional creatures. I found it hard to believe what I was finding. This discovery started me on a hunt for the truth behind the UFO/abductee phenomenon.

Figure 1: UFOs have abducted many humans.

Let's take the various myths of underground civilizations. There have been stories regarding this possibility for centuries. According to the most common myths, a race of advanced Elders sought sanctuary under the Earth in order to escape from some major catastrophe. Imagine my surprise when one or two of the abductees that I interviewed began to talk about their meetings with the advanced race of Elders in underground Alien bases.

Suspecting that the Abductees had made up these stories in order to gain publicity, I began to almost literally cross examine (after all I am an attorney) them on various minor points in their stories. I really didn't know what to say when not only did their stories mesh almost exactly, but they actually seemed to supplement each other's descriptions of the events, locations and medical procedures used. This was especially shocking considering that the two abductees in question did not known each other nor had there been any contact between the two prior to my examination of them.

I my examination, I tried to leave no stone unturned. I tried every method I knew short of lie detector tests to try and find flaws in the stories of the abductees. Even hypnosis failed to shake their stories. After completing the examination, I could only assume that they really believed what they were saying.

INTO THE UNKNOWN

As I continued my research, the trail led me deeper and deeper into what our modern world calls myths and the supernatural. I found that, while the trappings changed (i.e. people being abducted and taken on board flying saucers by men from outer space instead of people being kidnapped by gnomes and taken to underground cities populated by the Elders) much of the behavior exhibited by these "creatures" remained fairly constant. It appeared that, for centuries, the human race has been the target of some "forces" curiosity.

One of the most unusual interviews that I conducted was with a young lady who swore that she came from an Underground City. She told me that her name was Bonnie. She came to me through the assistance of a truly brilliant U.F.O. researcher named William Hamilton. A man of unquestionable character, he vouched for the young lady and confirmed much of what she had to say to me.

If she can be believed, and I could not punch a hole in her story, her father is the inner world's ambassador with the surface and she can travel the world through a series of ancient underground subway tunnels.

I found her entire story, which was repeated on my radio show, to be completely believable from the point of view that much of what she said, other than the existence of the underground city was confirmed. Among the facts that were confirmed was her ability to cover great distances in very short periods of time. This was allegedly due to her ability to use the underground shuttles referred to above.

Does Bonnie and her story prove the existence of an underground civilization? Certainly not, but it does open up an entire new series of questions and a new direction for research. Remember that truth is sometimes stranger than fiction.

EGO INTERFERENCE

Could all of these bizarre happenings (such as sightings and landing traces) be the result of swamp gas and the abductee stories be hoaxes and the ramblings of unbalanced people as our ivory tower inhabiting scientists were fond of saying? While I don't believe this to be the case, I felt that it was something that needed to be looked into in order to have completed a thorough study. Unfortunately, those laughingly called scientists were almost unanimous in refusing to even discuss the possibility that there might be anything to these stories. Talk about people with open minds.

Therefore, I tried to talk to some of the better known researchers in this field. To my sorrow, I found that, in many cases, the so-called U.F.O. experts were having trouble seeing past their egos. In fact, after I conducted a telephone interview of one of these "experts" on my show, I had the researcher later call me at my office and proceed to read me the riot act for not giving him the proper credit for some data that I had talked about on my show and worst of all, in his mind, I wasn't showing him what he felt was the proper deference as befitted his station.

In fact a great deal of what I found in this somewhat unusual field of research seemed to consist of various people trying to twist the available facts to fit their own pet theories.

A great deal of the data being put out by several supposedly serious sources seemed to be about fifty percent disinformation and fifty percent their own "insider information". I also found that disagreeing or daring to question the findings of these "experts" was a sure way of being attacked as a "government agent" or worse.

I also found that paranoia ran rampant. Now I will have to say in defense of the numerous paranoids that I met in the course of my work, that there is great reason to be paranoid in this particular field. (I will also observe that some of the worst paranoids were more open minded than many of the so-called "experts") From my own experience, I know that UFO researchers find their phones taped (my office phone was found to be taped by no less an authority than the phone company), their mail is diverted, delayed or never arrives (I was asked what I thought of the material they had sent me by several people I had never heard of before), offices and homes are entered and their files taken (some information was removed from my office by a person or persons unknown, nothing else was taken) and there are numerous mysterious telephone calls.

Additionally, and tragically, if any of these poor paranoid people seem to be achieving some success, there are numerous others who want to ride on their coat-tails. While I don't consider myself paranoid, (but after all even paranoids do have enemies), but I did have numerous problems with would-be actresses who wanted to use my show as a springboard to success and would-be air personalities who were stars in their own minds, who thought they were too important to help build a better show.

However, in spite of all the strangeness and obstacles placed in my path by people that I thought were friends, I resolved to do a book about the matter as I saw it. I vowed to avoid the paranoia that seemed to pervade the field.

HOLY SPACE BROTHERS

Unfortunately, as I began to put some flesh on my bare bones theory, I began to come across some of the most unbelievable information that I had ever seen. From researching Unidentified Flying Objects and so-called abductions, I found that I had to delve into various religious teachings as much of what the so-called aliens seemed to be saying had a religious bent. While studying religion, I found that I was constantly running into references to various secret societies and cults. A study of these little known organizations led me back through history to ancient Gods and Goddesses.

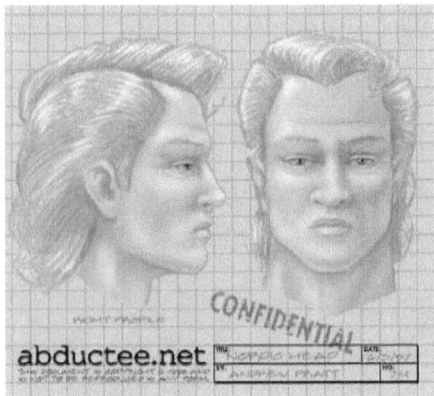

Figure 2: There are many stories of Nordic appearing aliens.

One theme that seemed to run throughout this entire field of research was the importance of religious belief. So I spent a great deal of time studying the various references and found that many of them were almost identical to teachings found in the Cult of Isis. This led me to theorize that the current crop of human abducting "Aliens" may have a connection with the ancient Gods and Goddesses of the Middle East.

"DOCTORED" HISTORY

Trying to put it all together, I found that in many cases, contemporary reports by little known writers painted an entirely different picture of historical events than did the accepted sources. As a result I was coming up with an entirely different picture of what had actually happened at various turning points in history that what history told us had happened. This, naturally, led me into taking a closer look at various historical reports.

To my utmost surprise, I found that most of what we

had been taught in school was not anywhere close to being correct. As an example, I could not find anyone, except a few confused researchers like myself, who had ever heard or read anything about the Czar of Russia sending troops and ships to help Abraham Lincoln fight the Civil War.

After coming across several of these types of historical omissions, I began to see that, perhaps, history had been changed to benefit some person or persons unknown or perhaps some political group. From this monumental discovery, it was only a short step to finding myself neck deep in what the liberal media laughingly calls the Conspiracy Theory of History.

I found that as I researched the material that became the first volume of THE OCCULT CONNECTION, that the Conspiracy Theory of History had a great deal of support when one took the trouble to check the facts. Unfortunately for society in general, those who should be checking the facts are too busy espousing the position of the Conspirators, since they have everything to gain and nothing to lose by siding with those in power. For example, what would orthodox historians do to an individual, or even one of their own, who tried to prove that Franklin D. Roosevelt actually knew of and looked forward to the attack on Pearl Harbor?

I also found, to my surprise, that many otherwise

intelligent people were ready to dismiss my book as ridiculous without bothering to even check my source material. I made very public challenges on the radio for anyone who desired to do so to appear on my program and debate me. I dared anyone who wanted to do so to come and prove me wrong. No one took me up on my challenge. However, the station was bought and the format changed so that the station only played Lawrence Welk music. So much for my show.

AN UNNECESSARY DEFENSE

Seldom do I feel it necessary to defend my actions, I generally take the position that a friend is going to believe that my intentions were good and an enemy is never going to be convinced that I did not act with evil intentions. However, in this particular instance, and as a result of some of the uproar caused by my first book, I will break my usual rule and explain the reasons I wrote the first volume of THE OCCULT CONNECTION: U.F.O.S, SECRET SOCIETIES AND ANCIENT GODS[1].

In spite of what some of my critics have had to say, I had no intention of trying to make anyone believe that there

---

[1] Hudnall, Ken, U.F.O.S, SECRET SOCIETIES AND ANCIENT GODS. Omega Press, Anaheim, CA. 1990.

is no GOD. Nor did I have any intention of attacking anyone's religious beliefs. Let me say for the fourth or fifth time that I do believe in GOD, however, believing in GOD does not, and should not, forbid one from exploring the legends and stories that clutter up the religious landscape. I was, and am, making a valid attempt to examine certain aspects of world history from a purely common sense point of view.

Much of our knowledge of the ancient world and the basis of many of our religious beliefs come from the ancient Sumerian writings. Therefore, I felt that in examining some of those writings, I could get an idea of the reality of some of our "Ancient Gods". I was correct, however, this examination appears to, inexplicably, have upset many people.

Next, I must point out that what I created in Book One of this series was a theory or a series of theories, if you prefer. Before one can arrive at any valid truth, there must be a theory, or a starting point from which to start any research. I will be the first to admit that my theory may sound outlandish to some, but simply because something sounds outlandish, doesn't mean it isn't true. I would suggest that to Americans living in 1934, the idea that in 35 years, men from America would walk on our Moon would have sounded just as outlandish.

So I began a study to try and answer several questions at one time. My foremost desire is to try and make some sort of sense out of the UFO mystery, and at the same time examine the impact that advanced beings may have had on the human race. Then, it is my intention to delve into the question of whether or not these same advanced beings may not still be manipulating us today.

For those who have not as of yet read Book One of this series, and at the risk of boring those who have read the first volume, I think it would be of value to repeat within this volume my theory in its entirety, the theory around which this entire series is built.

CHAPTER TWO

MY THEORY[2]

I am sure that you have wondered up to this point, exactly where I am going with this book. Well, I aim to show, at least, circumstantially, that it is entirely possible that this planet was colonized by a small group of settlers from another planet who still control much of what goes on from the shadows. . I don't think that they planned on staying as long as they have, but they were marooned here. Where that other planet might be shall be addressed as we progress. However, allow me to present my case.

First I want to list my main reference books. While I am sure that the skeptics among you will scoff that I am using third hand information, I want to challenge them to at least read the works that I am about to list. The problem with most skeptics is that they generally have absolutely no idea

---

[2] Hudnall, Ken, THE OCCULT CONNECTION,. Omega Press, Anaheim, Ca. 1990. Chapter 9, page 155.
(Reprinted in its' entirety from the first volume of this series)

what they are talking about when they denigrate a theory. It appears that they just like to flap their gums.

The authors of the modern works I have carefully researched. I have the greatest respect for their credentials. The ancient works that I use have been vouched for by literary minds much greater than mine, so I shall give respect to the works until they can be proven wrong.

Now one point that you must remember, as I remarked in the Preface to this work, I <u>DO BELIEVE IN GOD</u>, I just question whether some of the things attributed to HIM were performed by HIM. I find the idea of the GOD who created this marvelous planet being as petty as recorded in the Old Testament and in some of the legends as being unpalatable.

So before deciding that I am attacking your faith and therefore throw this book in the trash, at least do me the courtesy of hearing my theory in its' fullest.

References:
Works by Zecharia Sitchin
The 12th Planet
The Stairway To Heaven
The Wars of Gods and Men
The Lost Realms

Works by Christian O'Brien

The Megalithic Odyssey

The Genius of the Few

The King James Version of the Holy Bible

Translations of the Original Greek version of the Holy Bible

Translations of the Original Hebrew version of the Holy Scriptures

The Book of Mormon

The Book of Enoch

The Book of the Secrets of Enoch

Figure 3: Zecharia Sitchin

As you can see there are numerous works that I have used as references in compiling my theory. You might be surprised that not one of these works even came close to opposing my theory.

So without further ado, I present Hudnall's Theory of History.

Now understand, I am not an archeologist, nor an anthropologist. I have used reports written by the ancient scribes, so I may be wrong in details, but I believe that my overall picture is accurate.

> 1. *I believe it entirely possible that at some point, estimated to be some one half million years ago, a small band of colonists came to this planet.*

DATA: The arrival of the colonists pre-dated the earliest of man's written records. Zecharia Sitchin places their arrival at approximately 450,000 years ago, based on writings of the ancient Sumerians[3]. It is theorized that these visitors from another world came in search of silver and gold that was needed on their home world for scientific purposes. There is, of course, always the possibility that they were sent here to prepare this planet for resettlement by the rest of their race. For if their race is in dire trouble on their home planet, and this planet is suitable for them to survive on, then it would make since to prepare a new home for their race.

Other records of Sumerians call these visitors, *the Annanaki or Annanagi* depending on which theory you subscribe to, *the Lords of Cultivation,* since they first established farming as a task for man[4]. It is theorized that the Garden of Eden, of Biblical fame, was a colony established when they first arrived on this planet. The Garden was an

---

[3] Sitchin, Zecharia, THE WARS OF GODS AND MEN, Avon Books, New York. 1985.
[4] O'Brien, Christian, THE GENIUS OF THE FEW, Turnstone Press Limited, Wellingborough, Northamptonshire, G.B. 1985.

area where food was grown for consumption. History does seem to support the belief that the particular area of the Middle East was barren when the Annanaki first arrived.

>   2. *These colonists built an earth base, called Eden, from which they began to survey the planet.*

DATA: Christian O'Brien, in his book, THE GENIUS OF THE FEW, refers to the Book of Enoch for the name of the Garden. He states that "*At Kharsag, where Heaven and Earth met, the Heavenly Assembly, the Great Sons of Anu, descended--the many wise Ones*[5].

As stated by Sitchin in his works, ANU was the name, or title, of the Supreme Ruler of the Annanaki. Baalbek was built in his honor, as an Earth base for him.

>   3. *The concept of Heaven, in reality, referred to Eden, the Annanaki mountain base.*

DATA: The word from the original Hebrew that has been translated as 'the heavens' was ha'shemin. This Hebrew word is a plural form that actually means the skies. (3) The Hebrew word SHEM also means heights. SHM was also the root of a word meaning plant. Based on these clues, it is felt that the word ha'shemin actually meant the highlands, the

---

[5] Ibid

location of the Garden of Eden.[6]

> 4. *The colonists were physically bigger and stronger than earth man. Primitive man, less sophisticated than modern homo sapien, viewed these beings with awe.*

DATA: Using the story of the early Hebrews wandering in the desert, being led by *YAHWEH ELOHIM*, or *JEHOVAH*, as he has come to be known, it is possible to get some idea of the size of the ANNANAKI. From the construction of the tent that was built by Moses, (as a "home" for YAHWEH ELOHIM) it appears that *YAHWEH ELOHIM was approximately eight feet tall*[7].

As a result of the power demonstrated by these beings, early man followed them in child-like awe. The counsel and guidance of these beings gave rise to the first and most glorious civilization in history, the Sumerian Civilization.

> 5. *The colonists had some characteristic that made them give off a shine or glow from their skin.*

DATA: The Hebrew word EL is translated as God. However, *GOD is referred to as ELOHIM, the plural form, meaning Gods.* The Hebrew word EL came from the

---
[6] Ibid
[7] Ibid

Sumerian word EL which translates as brightness or shining. As a matter of fact, the Akkadians, the Babylonians, the Old Welsh, the Old Irish, the English and the Old Cornish all had words that were variations of the original EL and each of these variations meant shining or brightness[8]. This gives rise to the theory that the ancient writers were trying to describe a being that gave off a glow or a brightness.

> 6. *These colonists had the ability to fly, whether individually or by a craft.*

DATA: Almost every ancient writer talks of the Angels or the Annanaki being able to fly. Enoch talks of being taken up by them and taken to Heaven[9]. It has been said that early artists painted wings on Angels merely to show that they can fly.

> 7. The colonists were divided into two classes, the autocrats and the technicians.

DATA: The ancient Sumerian writings refer to the Annanaki who were laboring to carry out the orders of the Heavenly Council[10]. Others of the Annanaki were later sent

---

[8] Ibid
[9] The Book Of Enoch
[10] Sitchin, Zecharia, THE WARS OF GODS AND MEN, Avon Books, New York. 1985.

to the lowlands to teach mankind the skills of civilization.

> 8. *The colonists are very long lived, but also have the ability to extend their normal life spans to something approaching immortality.*

DATA: The patriarchs of the Bible all lived several hundred years. This infers one of two things. *Either man was originally genetically designed to live extended periods or that there was some artificial way of extending life.* The later seems the more probable.

In fact there is reference to the existence of a life extending substance both in the Bible[11] and in the ancient Sumerian Texts[12]. I might also point out that there is reference to this same substance in the legends of almost every civilization that existed on this earth. In Europe it was called ambrosia, the Nectar of the Gods. In the legends from India, Gilgamesh set off to ask for Immortality from the Supreme God. The implication is that this substance would also extend the life of man. If man and the Annanaki are genetically similar as we shall discuss later, then this would be quite likely.

A prime example of the existence of this substance

---

[11] THE HOLY BIBLE KING JAMES EDITION. The Book of Genesis.
[12] Sitchin, Zecharia, THE WARS OF GODS AND MEN. Avon Books, New York. 1985.

came from one of the Sumerian Texts, from which the later Book of Genesis was taken. In this text, the wording is as follows:

> *[Then did the Deity Yahweh say: "Behold, the Adam has become as one of us, to know good from Evil. And now might he not put forth his hand and partake also of the Tree of life, and eat, and live forever?" And the Deity Yahweh expelled the Adam from the orchard of Eden.]*[13]

This scene took place after Adam and Eve ate from the Tree of Knowledge. It would appear that the promise of eternal life was intended to be a physical eternal life and not a spiritual eternal life.

It also shows that the Annanaki had reason to fear man if man should be given the opportunity for eternal life. Could it be that the "gods" of the ancient world were not as all powerful as they would have it appear?

9. *The colonists established several bases throughout the Middle East.*

DATA: The ancient Sumerians write of the head of the Gods, called ENLIL, as establishing several centers. The

---

[13] O'Brien, Christian, <u>THE GENIUS OF THE FEW</u>, Turnstone Press Limited, Wellingborough, Northamptonshire, G.B., 1985

"gods" established the cities of Eridu, Larsa, Nippur, Bad-Tibira, Lark, Sippar, Shuruppak, and Lagash. Each of these cities served a certain function[14].

> 10. *The autocrats, which include the scientists, manipulate the weather to give them a longer growing season for crops.*

DATA: The ancient writers speak of the "gods" making the rains come and causing crops to grow. This has been a belief of almost every race on this planet. After all, ENLIL was also known as the Lord of Cultivation[15].

> 11. *The technician class was forced to do all the heavy labor. This resulted in a mutiny[16]. The head of the science team was ordered by the mission commander to see if it was possible to train indigenous man to work in place of the technicians. It was found that ape-man was not a suitable worker.*

DATA: Both Sitchin and O'Brien report on the Sumerian writings regarding the unhappiness of the Annanaki who were forced to do manual labor. It is interesting to note that while the two researchers differ on

---
[14] Ibid
[15] Ibid
[16] Sitchin, Zecharia, THE WARS OF GODS AND MEN. Avon Books, New York. 1985.

how they view what they found in the ancient records, their overall interpretations arrive at the same point.

The ancient Sumerian writings, the Epic of Creation, point to this mutiny of the lesser Annanaki as being the reason for the creation of man. Mankind was designed and created to serve the masters, the Annanaki[17].

> 12. *On orders of the mission commander, which the approval of the overall commander, a program of genetic manipulation was undertaken, to find a suitable worker drone.*

DATA: Many researchers have puzzled over the statements attributed to GOD in the Bible, such as "*Let us make man in our image.*" The basic question is, if there is and was only one God, then who was God talking to? According to the Sumerian writings, the Annanaki had to finally mix the sperm of an Annanaki with the ova of an ape-woman and then had it placed in the womb of female Annanaki volunteers. Eventually, man was created[18].

> 13. *Several genetic programs were undertaken to find the perfect worker. One involved taking the egg of a reptile, this was found not to be suitable, and the resulting creature was turned out of*

---
[17] Ibid
[18] Ibid

Eden.

DATA: There have been several articles written by anthropologists theorizing what a reptilian humanoid would look like. Eventually several skeletons were found that confirmed the theories. These skeletons were dated as being as old, if not more so, than the oldest human skeleton[19].

> 14. *It was found that mammals, the ape specifically, were best suited to genetic manipulation.*

DATA: It is apparent that the Annanaki were themselves, mammalian in genetic make-up since they could breed with human females[20]. *"And the sons of God saw the daughters of man and took them to wife."*

> 15. *Ape man, Neanderthal, and Cro-Magnon man were all results of these genetic manipulation programs. None of these species were entirely suitable.*

DATA: The theories of Charles Darwin propose that modern man is the result of changes in the makeup of various stages of human development such as Ape man to Neanderthal. However, science has discovered that at one

---

[19] Weekly World News
[20] THE BOOK OF ENOCH AND THE HOLY BIBLE.

point in history, several different "models" of human existed at the same time. Therefore, it appears to be improbable that one developed from the other. The most probable answer would be a genetic manipulation program. Such a genetic manipulation program could also explain how the various racial differences came into being.

> 16. *Finally, it was decided to take the sperm of one of the colonists and mix it with the eggs of a Cro-Magnon woman. The fertilized ovary was then implanted in the womb of a colonist female. The result was homo-sapien.*

DATA: This is thoroughly explained in the Epic of Creation, one of the Sumerian Epics[21].

> 17. *Man being a hybrid was sterile. However, in order not to have to waste precious genetic material, man was given the ability to procreate. This ability to procreate was perhaps unauthorized, but once the damage was done, the commander accepted it.*

DATA: This is also touched on in the Epic of Creation and other Sumerian and Akkadian writings[22].

---

[21] Sitchin, Zecharia, <u>THE WARS OF GODS AND MEN</u>, Avon Books, New York. 1985.
[22] Ibid

18. *Man, being genetically close to the colonists is able to have his life extended in the same manner as the colonists.*

DATA: Already discussed in #8 above.

19. *Man originally began life as a servant in Eden, farming the "Garden".*

DATA: The original twelve couples who were the patriarchs of the Bible were placed in the Garden according to both the Scriptures and the Sumerian Texts. It was only when Adam and Eve disobeyed that they were turned out of the Garden. Later, when the Human Race became too many to comfortably fit in the Garden, that many, the excess if you will, were resettled onto the plains nearby[23].

20. *When the number of humans became too many to be comfortably held in Eden, tribes, or settlements, were established on the plains below the mountains in which Eden lay.*

DATA: According to the Sumerian Texts, the Gods established the cities of the Sumerian Civilization. Each "God" had his, or her, own city state, all loosely under the control of the Heavenly Assembly.

---

[23] O'Brien, Christian, THE GENIUS OF THE FEW, Turnstone Press Limited, Wellingborough, Northamptonshire, G.B., 1985

> 21. *The technician class was becoming rebellious and caused certain of the plans of the autocrats to go awry. For example, it is recorded in the Sumerian legends that it was one of the Watchers (See 23) that tempted Eve. It appears that he tempted her to eat the material that resulted in mind expansion, i.e., the knowledge of good and evil, and perhaps, extended life. An act strictly against the rules.*

DATA: According to the Book of Enoch, the "junior gods" were sent out from Eden to teach and watch the developing human race. These teachers, or the Watchers as they were called (the IGIGI in the original Sumerian) were apparently all male and were tempted by the Human females. As a result, the Watchers broke their orders of non-interference and took human females as wives. They also proceeded to teach the human race ideas that they were not intended to know.

It is also interesting to know that the Watchers were called Serpents. Thus was Eve tempted by a Serpent, a man of the Serpent Order, not a talking reptile.

> 22. *Eating the material that extended life also seems to have had the effect of sharpening mental powers, making Adam and Eve aware of their nakedness. The numerically smaller colonists rightly feared man's awakening mental state and*

> *exiled the two transgressors to the outside world. The guards had orders not to let them back into the Garden.*

DATA: If Eden was a colony, it had an entrance. Once Adam and Eve were exiled from the Garden, or the colony, the security guards had orders not to let them back inside the colony. It was probably feared that they would "contaminate" the rest of the human race[24].

> 23. *The technicians were sent down to the plains to study the development of man and to make sure that everything went according to plan. Such an act also kept them from causing mischief in Eden.*

DATA: It was the Watchers, or the technician class, who had earlier rebelled against the senior Annanaki[25]. Therefore, the safest course of action would have been to have sent the more aggressive of the Watchers out into the world to keep an eye on the burgeoning human race. It would also serve double duty in that it would keep the Watchers from being able to plot amongst themselves and cause more trouble in Eden[26].

---

[24] Ibid
[25] Sitchin, Zecharia, THE WARS OF GODS AND MEN, Avon Books, New York. 1985.
[26] O'Brien, Christian, THE GENIUS OF THE FEW, Turnstone Press Limited, Wellingborough, Northamptonshire, G.B., 1985

24. *These technicians, called the Watchers by Enoch since their job was to watch the human race, were lonely and took human females as wife. These unions produced monstrous children.*

DATA: This is verified in the Bible, the Book of Enoch, the Sumerian and the Akkadian Writings. The Sons of God saw that the daughters of man were fair and took them to wife[27]. From these unions children were born who became man of renown in days of old. It is recorded that these children grew into monsters who proceeded to rape and pillage the land[28].

25. *Certain humans were taken and trained to be agents of the colonists among the developing tribes. Enoch was one.*

DATA: Several times in the Bible, it is recorded that certain of the patriarchs did not die, but were taken up by God to walk with God. Among these were Elisah and Enoch[29]. It is also possible that Moses was so taken.

In the Book of Enoch, the true story of what happened to one of these who was taken by God is told. Enoch was trained to be a scribe and a liaison from the Heaven Assembly. What is told in the Book of Enoch is the

---
[27] THE HOLY BIBLE, KING JAMES EDITION.
[28] The Book of Enoch
[29] Ibid

tale of a primitive man who is taken up by an advanced race of beings and trained to be their servant.

> 26. *Angered at the actions of the technicians, the autocrats sent a human emissary, Enoch, to inform them of their punishments.*

DATA: In the Book of Enoch, Enoch talks of the anger of the Gods at the acts of the Watchers. He is sent to tell the Watchers of their punishments. The Watchers try and get Enoch to be their defense attorney in their upcoming trial in absentia[30].

> 27. *Colonial law enforcement personnel were sent to arrest the Watchers. The offending colonists were imprisoned in underground caverns.*

DATA: The area around Eden was rift with several ravines and caverns. Since these Watchers were almost immortal as a result of their extended life spans, the best that the Annanaki Council could do would be to imprison them until they could be transported to the home planet for trial[31].

> 28. *In order to protect the gene pool of the developing Human Race, the colonial commander had all the human families of the offending Watchers killed. This served the double*

---

[30] Ibid
[31] Ibid

> *duty of stopping the spread of advanced technological information that the Watchers had revealed and also stopped the disruption of the normal development of the gene pool of the Human Race[32].*

DATA: The head of the Annanaki seemed unusually angry at the action of the Watchers. More than such a transgression would appear to warrant. Granted, it might appear to be similar to the way that we would view bestiality, since they appeared to view the developing Human Race as something to be used or as a tool, but certainly it would not be something that should warrant such treatment. It seems that the Annanaki were willing to be unmerciful to anything that would affect the genetic structure of the new race.

Therefore, it had to be a transgression that was considered extremely serious to warrant the mass death and destruction that took place in order to wipe out the human families of the offending Watchers.

> 29. *A sympathetic technician working in the scientific section helped the imprisoned Watchers plan a jail break. It was planned that the break would be covered by an artificially generated storm.*

DATA: According to the information presented in Christian O'Brien's work, THE GENIUS OF THE FEW, Eden was

---

[32] Ibid

destroyed by a storm such as this planet had never seen[33]. During the Vietnam War, the CIA experimented with weather control in order to cause flooding in the North. It backfired and resulted in flooding that threatened to cause harm in the South. It was also the reason that the P.O.W. camp that was raided at Son Tay was evacuated by the North Vietnamese.

Several of the written works by the Sumerians make it evident that the Annanaki were able to affect the weather.

> 30. *The storm allowed the Watchers to escape, but the technician who generated the covering storm miscalculated and the ensuing storm totally destroyed Eden and resulted in a major flood that covered most of the surrounding area.*

DATA: See #29 above[34].

> 31. *The Watchers escaped, swearing revenge for the death of their families.*

DATA: It is evident that the Watchers escaped for their remains have never been found in the areas where they were imprisoned. It would suppose the need for revenge as it would be a natural feeling after having your family

---

[33] O'Brien, Christian, THE GENIUS OF THE FEW, Turnstone Press Limited, Wellingborough, Northamptonshire, G.B., 1985
[34] Ibid

destroyed for no good reason. The Annanaki seemed to exhibit much of the same moods as we Humans show.

> 32. *The two competing groups, the autocrats and the Watchers are locked in a struggle for control of the planet.*

DATA: This is supposition, but some of the names of the Watchers given in the Book of Enoch are the same of similar as the names of some of the followers of Satan. This would explain the battle between "Good and Evil" and the "Sons of the Light against the Powers of the Dark". The prize seems to be either the control of men in some physical manner or else control of this planet as a whole[35].

> 33. *The Watchers have become known as the Legions of Satan.*

DATA: As pointed out above, the names of Satan's demons are the same or similar as names of the Watchers. The Watchers were also "thrown out of Heaven" so to speak, in that they were first more or less exiled to the plains and then forced to escape[36].

---

[35] Prophet, Elizabeth Clare, FORBIDDEN MYSTERIES OF ENOCH, Summit University Press, Livingston, MT. 1983.
[36] Ibid

34. *The autocrats have become known as the Angels of the Lord.*

DATA: According to the writings of the ancient Sumerians, such names as Michael and Gabriel were senior members of the Host who served God. Therefore, we can identify the senior Annanaki as those who are considered to be the power of light[37].

35. *Over the ensuing eons of time, both groups have lost their ability to support interstellar travel and can, at best, move around the solar system.*

DATA: The ancient writings also talk of a war that broke out between two factions of the "good gods". The prize was allegedly the space base located in the Sinai. One side is supposed to have used a mighty weapon that sounds suspiciously like a nuclear bomb to destroy the base so that the other side could not gain control of it. I would venture to guess that this destroyed a lot of irreplaceable equipment and may have marooned them here.

36. *The Watchers have established bases on, and in, the Earth.*

DATA: Many of the legends of earlier times maintain that

---

[37] Ibid

such things as Imps, Trolls, Dwarfs and Fairies lived underground in caves and caverns. I would be willing to bet that these creatures were the Watchers, mutated by the radiation fields of this Planet. These levels of radiation were in all likelihood different from what they were accustomed to. I would venture to guess that the Tree of Life in the Garden helped offset this problem. Without the benefits of this Tree, they may have begun to mutate.

> 37. *The autocrats, and probably the Watchers as well, have established bases in other parts of the solar system.*

DATA: I would point to the giant face and the ruined city on Mars as reported by Richard C. Hoagland in his book, The Monuments of Mars: A City on the Edge of Forever as partial proof. Some unknown race built a massive face and a city that consisted of architecture similar to that found in ancient Egypt[38]. In addition, several photographs of the surface of the Moon have shown what appear to be structures on the Moon's surface[39].

---

[38] Hoagland, Robert C., THE MONUMENTS OF MARS: A CITY ON THE EDGE OF FOREVER. North Atlantic Books, Berkeley, CA. 1987.
[39] Steckling, Fred, WE DISCOVERED ALIEN BASES ON THE MOON.

> 38. *Originally, both groups controlled man through the establishment of religions. As man become more sophisticated, this control method lost its usefulness.*

DATA: I am not sure that religion was the original reason behind the establishment of the priesthood. I would assume that such powerful beings as the Annanaki showed themselves to have massive egos as well. For this reason, I would suppose that the Annanaki felt it necessary to have many servants. These servants would be trained in the proper care and feeding of Gods. It would only be natural to use the servants as a method of talking to the common men. This later became modified, once the "Gods" no longer wished to rule directly, to the demi-god priest kings. Then later became the rule of the strongest with the Priests dealing only with the words of the gods[40].

> 39. *Originally, half-breed offspring of the "Gods" were set up as the secular rulers of man.*

DATA: Historically, Demi-gods, half man-half god, ruled prior to the dawn of modern history. Demi-gods were allegedly the off-spring of the union of God and Human.

---

[40] Sitchin, Zecharia, THE WARS OF GODS AND MEN, Avon Books, New York. 1985.

> 40. Secret societies *were established, where certain initiated individuals were given directions by the "gods" in how to manipulate their fellow men.*

DATA: Probably the first secret societies were the priests, who were taught much "secret" knowledge by the Gods. The later secret societies were probably made up of the followers of the various Dark Gods. In other words, those who gave allegiance to the Watchers.

> 41. *For some reason, between roughly A.D. 200 and A.D. 1990, the "gods" were unable to remain among us as rulers.*

DATA: It is theorized that sometime around 2,000 B.C. a nuclear war took place between two groups of Gods. This event is recorded in the writings of many civilizations of the ancient world. Even descriptions of the destruction of Sodom and Gomorrah appear to be the result of a rocket attack[41].

It is also theorized that the fallout cloud from the destruction of the space port was carried by the wind to Sumeria where it killed many. It is also reported that the Gods fled the fallout. This would imply that they were not totally immortal since they could apparently die from

---

[41] Ibid

radiation[42].

During this period, according to Sitchin's work, The Lost Realms[43] some of the Gods of the ancient world turned up in the Americas where they proceeded to establish civilization. The original architects of civilization in South America appear to be white, human appearing, men. This original civilization was destroyed by barbarians after the "Gods" left for their homelands.

> 42. *Through certain artificially created beings, the "gods" have continued to carry out the genetic experiments that began with the creation of early man.*

DATA: Several abductees who have had close contact with the "Greys", as well as, several prominent researchers have come to the conclusion that these creatures may be genetic constructs designed to operate in our environment. It is evident from their controlled jerky almost choreographed movements that they do not have the same type of free will that Humans demonstrate.

It is also evident from abductee reports that the "Greys" either conduct limited procedures in the bedroom or take the abductee to ships or bases where other, more expert

---
[42] Ibid
[43] Sitchin, Zecharia, <u>THE LOST REALMS</u>, Avon Books, New York. 1989.,

personnel, perform more complicated medical procedures. Perhaps the "Greys" are sophisticated androids that can follow simple programming, but have to contact higher headquarters if faced with unexpected resistance.

> 43. *Through these same artificially created beings, the "gods" have been making "deals" with various world governments in order to pave the way for their return.*

DATA: Again, this refers to the alleged treaty between the aliens and the U.S. Government. It is alleged that members of the U.S. Air Force met with the Aliens at Holloman Air Force Base and signed a treaty[44]. Certain financially powerful humans have assisted the "gods" in creating their desired world order in return for promises of power.

DATA: Refers to the secret societies that have assisted in trying to create a one world government, an apparent requirement of the "Gods"[45]. More on this in a later chapter.

> 44. *Each side of this "War of the Immortals" is attempting to mass a human following for a final confrontation. Only one side of this war will survive.*

---

[44] Cooper, Milton Williams, OPERATION MAJORITY.
[45] Allen, Gary and Larry Abrahamson., NONE DARE CALL IT CONSPIRACY. Double A Publications, Seattle, Washington.

DATA: According to reports from several abductees, the aliens are now starting to conduct dialogues with their victims. Such terms as "Will you follow us?" are used in the discussions. Religion is brought into the situation more and more. Even the final "confrontation" has been mentioned[46]. The major question is, who are the good guys?

A DISCUSSION OF MY THEORY

So now you have seen the basis of my theory. I believe that these Annanaki have come down to us reported as ancient Gods. The glowing characteristics of the entities, reported in the Book of Enoch, and elsewhere, are identical to those reported in such instances as the miracle at Fatima. Alleged miracles, such as the one at Fatima, have been used down through the ages to influence the direction in which civilization has been moving. When it appears that mankind is moving in a way that the "Gods" do not approve of, then along comes a "miracle", or a very charismatic leader that takes mankind back into the path approved of by these "Gods".

Due to the small number of these Annanaki that originally came here, they aren't strong enough to dominate a

---

[46] Fowler, Raymond, THE ANDREASSON AFFAIR, Bantam Books, New York. 1980.

sophisticated race; they can openly dominate only primitive tribes. As an example, when mankind and civilization was in its' infancy, the "Gods" moved among us openly as our direct rulers. As mankind became more sophisticated, then the "Gods" became more distant. Obviously, these "Gods" fear us as much as we have come to fear them.

A prime example of their desire to keep civilization disrupted and the humans fighting among ourselves it the sage of the Tower of Babel. Allegedly, this tower was built to allow man to strive for the power and the same level as the "Gods". As a response, the "Gods" confused the languages of man so that they were no longer able to work as a cohesive whole. This confusing of languages has led to eternal bloodshed and wars. Hardly the acts of benevolent "Gods".

These so-called "Gods" fear us and our potential. They fear us so much that they no longer walk among us, but work from a distance with a kind of remote control. In addition to, or perhaps because of, the fear that they have for us, they are few in number. It was reported by the ancient Sumerian records that less than a thousand of these "Gods" came to this planet. With so few of their own race on this planet, it is no wonder that they began to interbreed with Homo Sapien man.

As a result, in order to control so many humans, the Annanaki found that it was necessary that they utilize human fifth columnists to make up for their small numbers. The first of these human fifth columnists are those who have started the original secret society that gave rise to all of the others that are attempting to control the world.

I would believe, since the Sumerian records so report, that some of the Annanaki can pass among us without too much concern of detection by ordinary humans. These are the ones who act as liaison with the secret societies. Others, less "human looking" control the abduction crews that man the silver disks.

It is my contention that the small pasty white aliens who move in unison are actual genetic constructs that are under the mental control of the leader of the team. They are either genetic constructs or temporary bodies being operated by computer controlled intelligences. The implants, allegedly placed in each of the abductees, are probably a device to make mental control possible or easier.

The war between the Watchers and the Gods continues to this day. But instead of open combat, with pawn countries fighting in the name of religion or some other allegedly "holy" purpose, it is more like a behind the scenes war. Each side strives to build more followers for the big day when the next open warfare does breakout. All of these battles build up to what most religions call "The day of Armageddon" or what we call the Last Battle. For on this day, the Gods of the ancient world return.

In discussing these ancient Gods, there are certain questions that I am sure that you would like to ask. In fact, as I have talked to many people, they have all asked similar questions. The main questions have been:

- Where did the "Gods" go when they disappeared?
- Why did they leave? and
- What have they been up to over the last few thousand of our years?

I touched on some of the answers to these questions when I discussed my theory. This theory was the basis of Volume I of this series[47]. In Volume I, I expanded the theory greatly and showed various common aspects between the U.F.O.s that seemingly fill out night skies, the above referenced secret societies and the Ancient gods of history. I pointed to several common threads of teachings promoted by all three. The reactions of the readers have been both gratifying and totally puzzling.

Most have said once they picked up the book and

---

[47] Hudnall, Ken, THE OCCULT CONNECTION, U.F.O.s, Secret Societies and Ancient Gods, Omega, Anaheim, CA. 1990.

actually started to read it, they couldn't put it down. Some have bought more than one copy in order to given copies to their friends. Several have reported thefts of the book by their friends who couldn't put the book down. Such reports make any author feel good that people like his writing style. However as I said earlier, some reactions have puzzled me. Below are three of the puzzling reactions.

THEY ARE GOING TO GET YOU!

The reaction that most amuses me is the one where the reader is sure that because I am putting out what they feel is, or should be, classified information that the forces of silence are going to remove me. I submit that such a removal would be the best proof that what I am saying is true. Of course, it is always pointed out that such a method of proving my theory would not be conducive to a long career in writing, which is true.

I am not delving into classified files of any particular service and revealing information that would make it a certainty that we would all be speaking Russian by next Thursday. What I am doing is taking information that is released to the public, but not given wide coverage, together with information furnished me by various contacts and showing how it fits into a pattern. This pattern shows a plan that is worse for the human race than a mere conquering by a foreign power.

YOU REPRESENT THE FORCES OF SATAN!

Since the publication of the first book of this series, I have had many come to debate my theory, each all puffed up with his or her "God-given" power to banish the forces of darkness. It is amazing that if one merely raises questions regarding organized religion, then it is assumed that the one who raises the questions is anti-God. I find it puzzling that some of the same people, who make it a point to examine everything of every angle before making a decision, immediately yell anti-God when religion is questioned. There seems to be something wrong with this picture.

I have been no different from other authors of book of this type. I have been inundated by kooks and detractors of all description. My favorite was the little old lady with the flower in her hat. She was simply the nicest lady I have ever met. She reminded me so much of my own grandmother that even though she annoyed me no end, I simply couldn't get mad at her. Unfortunately, she was so sure that I was sent here by Satan to lead people from the "true" path that she couldn't really concentrate on my logic, but instead, sat with her back to the door and appeared ready to run at the first sign that I was changing into SATAN.

I debated with this little old lady for over an hour with her quoting scripture until she was totally out of breath. I think that it confused her that for every scriptural quote she gave me, I gave her one that proved my point. (For those fundamentalists who call and quote scripture over the phone and then hang up, I do know something about the Bible.)

After another hour of seriously discussing my theory with an open mind, she finally admitted that I raised some points that she couldn't find answers for in her Bible. I think that we parted as friends, but I'm not sure.

IF IT'S TRUE WHY DOESN'T OUR GOVERNMENT DO SOMETHING ABOUT IT?

Then there are the super patriots and the "let's not talk about bad things" groups. Both of these groups take the position that the U.S. Government can do no wrong and will always look out for its citizens. It is those who have this viewpoint that find it the hardest to adjust to the truth. These groups are also the ones who react the most violently when I answer their questions and then expound on my views in this area.

They simply find it impossible to believe that our government doesn't do something about the conspiracy because our government is part of it. In spite of their denials, the evidence is very convincing that our government has been infiltrated by the very forces that I write about. In fact it is to thoroughly examine this question that I have written this particular book in the series.

However, before moving on, let me once again answer the main questions of most:

- *I do believe in God.*
- *I also believe that there is a major conspiracy underway.*
- *I do believe in our system of government, but not necessarily in the manner in which it is being operated.*
- *I will continue to believe in my theory until such time as someone can show me a fallacy in it.*

AND I DO CHALLENGE ANYONE TO FIND A FLAW IN MY THEORY. IF I AM WRONG, SHOW ME!

THE CONPIRACY

In Volume One of the Occult Connection, I had originally started out to write a book about Unidentified Flying Objects, but somehow in the midst of this endeavor, I stumbled across many other matters that seemed, at least to me, to be directly involved. Most have now heard about the MJ-12 scenario, where there is, allegedly, an organization that was put together by one of our earlier Presidents charged with dealing with the Aliens. From this, admittedly farfetched conspiracy of silence, I began to investigate many apparently unrelated areas. The result was a theory even more unbelievable than Aliens visiting this Planet and abducting females. I discovered, interconnected with various aspects of the UFO puzzle, what appeared, to me, to be a signs of a larger conspiracy that seemed to run back into the mists of time. It's goal, world domination.

Is such a thing possible, could there actually be a few families that have dedicated themselves to a centuries' long program of domination and destruction? I had to find out. Therefore, I began to delve deeper and deeper into the various conspiracy theories that seemed to litter the landscape. To my amazement, I found that I could construct a logical conspiracy theory that would account for many, heretofore, puzzling aspects of world politics and also account for some extremely bizarre behavior exhibited by many of our politicians. Worst of all, it also seemed to account for the steady decline of our own great land.

Many people have no idea what is going on behind the scenes in this country. We have grown up being taught that our government is a government of the people, by the people and for the people. Once this was true, but in the early part of this century, this changed to read a government of the Conspiracy, by the Conspiracy and for the Conspiracy.

COINCIDENCE?

To really believe what I am about to write will make you a deadly enemy to the liberal media in this country. According to the national media, the written press especially, everything bad in the world just happens; there is no master plan to world events. In fact, if you want to make an enemy of a liberal, tell him, or her that you subscribe to the conspiracy theory of history. Any liberal worth his salt will point out that a conspiracy such as this proposes would have to be worldwide and span centuries. It will be quickly pointed out that such things just simply don't happen, then the tired old excuses of "It's all the fault of capitalism" or other such liberal tripe will fill your ears as he or she begins to warm to their favorite topic.

The liberal establishment wants you to believe that the mere fact that almost every ally that we have sworn to protect from the RED MENACE, (a former name for Communism, for those of you raised and educated by the liberal establishment) has eventually been taken over by Communists must be just a coincidence. I must admit, however, that I, for one, subscribe to the James Bond School of Reasoning.

WHERE IS JAMES BOND WHEN WE NEED HIM?

It was Ian Fleming's fictional character, James Bond who proposed the school of thought that I find the most logical.

"If it happens once it is happenstance. If it happens twice, it is coincidence. If it happens three times, it is enemy action."

The truth is that almost every time that our State Department tries to prop up or support a friendly government, said friendly government goes Communist. This has happened far more than three times; actually it has happened over forty times since World War II. Every small Communist country that we try to oppose suddenly receives a stream of money, technology and assistance from unknown sources. Allegedly this steady stream of resources and backing comes from the Soviet Union, but let's face it, the Soviet Union's economy has been a shambles for several years. Where does the Soviet Union get the funds to support over a third of the world? This has also happened far more than three times. Can some other agency or entity be supporting the Soviet Union's conquests?

In order to give the reader a frame of reference for these happenings and in order to show the seriousness of these acts, in a later chapter we will discuss some of these "coincidences".

TREASON

I am sure that it has long been evident to the mysterious "controllers" who direct the conspiracy, that if the Conspiracy can control the United States then the Conspiracy can control the world. America seems to be a hard nut to crack for these "Controllers". For whatever reason, they have had to move very slowly in their conquest. It has been America and the strength of its people that have stopped the move for world domination in two world wars. So it soon became obvious that militarily, at least, America was a major problem for the one worlders. So other ways had to be found to control this country.

In spite of the liberal establishment's attempts to ignore the more obvious signs of a move afoot to control this country, a thorough study of history reveals diligent efforts have actually been made to control this country. As was observed by Adam Weishaupt, the alleged founder of the

Illuminati, to control an organization or a country, one does not have to use force of arms. A smarter, more subtle way is to control the leaders. As we progress, see if you don't agree with me that this appears to be what has happened to this Country.

In a later chapter, as we study some of our State Department's so-called errors in diplomacy, we can begin to get a glimpse of the "big picture" of treason and betrayal.

The effect of the treason is obvious. If our country can undermine the governments of our allies, then it is easier for agents of the Conspiracy to take these governments over. History shows that one after another we have, indeed, betrayed our allies and turned them over to the enemy. We do it so consistently that it couldn't be accidental, it can only be intentional. So then, why do our own elected leaders seek to work to our detriment? Is it intentional or accidental? Who are these leaders and what are their backgrounds? Could their actions be part of a much broader conspiracy? If there is a broad based conspiracy, then what is its' purpose?

As we try to answer these questions, let us first study some of the evidence that there really exists a conspiracy that has spanned eons. Can we really determine if there actually exist hidden "Masters" that work to keep mankind under control? Are we really being manipulated or are we just happily killing ourselves for nothing? As we try and answer these questions, settle back and get ready for the next installment of **THE OCCULT CONNECTION** as we try to look into the **ETERNAL CONSPIRACY.**

CHAPTER THREE

THE ETERNAL CONSPIRACY

There has been new data that has been discovered impacting on Book One in this series. For this reason, it is felt that an update is required. A lot of research has shown that there is actually an eternal conspiracy which is being run by figures from the shadows. I call them the Shadow Rulers.

Along with the so-called "New Age" of new political world order, there is now newly available information regarding a parallel religious "New Age". It would seem that the forces of the conspiracy are not just content with changing the way we govern ourselves, but they also desire to control the way that we worship our God. There seems to be a move afoot to create a "New Religious Order".

This religious "New World Order" was addressed by Manley P. Hall in his book, *LECTURES ON ANCIENT*

PHILOSOPHY[48], wrote:

> "A new light is breaking in the east; a more glorious day is at hand. The rule of the philosophic elect - the dream of the ages - will yet be realized and is not too far distant."

Another writer, Alice Bailey, in her book, *THE EXTERNALISATION OF THE HIERARCHY*[49], wrote:

> "Eventually, there will appear the Church Universal, and its definite outlines will appear towards the close of this century."

I would point out that we are now in the second decade of the 21st century and a lot of what I have written about has come to pass as we will discuss in this book. One only has to look at the daily newspapers or listen to the news broadcasts to see the truth of these statements. There seems to be numerous new religions springing up all across the world as more and more people become dissatisfied with the old religions and the old orders.

Christianity seems to find itself in somewhat the same position as the pagan religions did thousands of years ago, as more and more former members defect for the

---

[48] Hall, Manley P., LECTURES ON ANCIENT PHILOSOPHY, The Philosophical Research Society, Inc. L.A. 1984.
[49] Bailey, Alice, THE EXTERNALISATION OF THE HEIRARCHY, The Lucis Publishing Co. New York.

promises of the new "Gods". Even Satan seems to have found a fertile recruiting ground for new members as Satanic Cults spring up in some of our most religious countries.

Some have even turned the teachings of Christianity, itself, into a basis for new orders, such as the Aryan Nations Groups and the so-called Christian Identity religions[50]. Once again, an organized religion is being used as the spring broad to breed hate and contempt for others.

A METHOD OF DIVISION

What do these new religions or orders accomplish? They do not have the broad based appeal that Christianity did, and their message is usually one of hate. So what is the attraction that they hold out for new members?

Historically, it is during the declining years of a civilization that men seek new gods and new beliefs and insanity seems to run rampant. There have been many civilizations prior to our own. For example in the last days of the Roman Empire, numerous new religions sprang into existence, such as Christianity. In fact, these "new" religions was one of the contributing factors to the destruction of the old order. Today, we also have numerous "new" religions

---

[50] Flynn, Kevin and Gary Gerhardt, THE SILENT BROTHERHOOD, Signet Books, New York. 1989.

that want to tear down the existing order in order to install their own version of paradise. Will we go the way of the Roman Empire?

It is my belief that behind each and every one of the major changes of history has been this mysterious organization that I call the conspiracy. They are just as active today as they were a thousand years ago. They have always been with us, manipulating things form behind the scenes. Causing death and destruction to untold millions in order to tighten their control a little here and there and to make a profit.

THE NEW RELIGION

What are the tenets of this New Age Faith? What will the new religion preach? What kind of God will the new religion member worship?

In her book, *THE HIDDEN DANGERS OF THE RAINBOW*[51], Constance Cumbey discussed the beliefs of this new religion. According to Mrs. Cumbey, the new religion will have the following tenets:

- There will be a new Messiah, a World Government and a new world religion under the control of a Pope like figure named Maitreya.

---

[51] Cumbey, Constance, THE HIDDEN DANGERS OF THE RAINBOW, Huntington House, Inc. Shreveport, LA. 1983.

- Instead of a cash economy, there will be a universal credit card system.
- All of the world's food supply will be consolidated under one authority.
- The will be a worldwide tax system.
- There will be a worldwide draft.
  Christianity will be stamped out and its adherents will be exterminated.

Rather than examine each of these tenets here, as we progress through the book, keep these tenets in mind and see if there is not evidence that a move is afoot to put these into operation. You might be surprised regarding the identities of some of the supporters of these concepts.

However, keep in mind that the Conspiracy has long advocated the extermination of Christianity and the re-establishment of a Pantheistic Religion, which would be a religious counterpart to the collectivist type political environment that the Conspiracy desires. So it comes as little wonder that a new "Religious Age" is on the horizon.

CHAPTER FOUR

THE UNSEEN MASTERS

"An invisible hand is guiding the populace."
Lafayette

So in keeping with the basic premise of the Occult Connection Series, the question must be asked: where do Secret Societies fit into the scheme of things in so far as Unidentified Flying Objects are concerned?

I have no intention to bore the reader, but a quick review is necessary at this point. My theory proposes the following points:

- Advanced beings colonized this planet eons ago.
- These advanced beings were looked at as "Gods" by various religions and were responsible for creating what became the human race.
- These advanced beings taught us the rudiments of civilized living and directly ruled over human cities.

- The humans who directly served the "Gods", called naturally, the Servants of God, acted as intermediaries between the "Gods" and the common man.
- The "Gods" had a falling out among themselves and a civil war resulted. In this civil war, human pawns fought the battles of the "Gods". Nuclear weapons were used in these battles.
- For some reason the "Gods" were forced to withdraw from direct contact with mankind. They left half breed offspring in their place as a new race of "demi-Gods" to rule over mankind, with the "Servants of the Gods" as assistants.
- The "demi-Gods" died out or left to join their parents. This left the "Priest-Kings" to rule over the human race as the direct representatives of the "Gods". The Priest Kings, in turn, were replaced by secular rulers. This began the struggle between religion (the priests) and government (the King). Behind the scenes were the "Gods" who have continued to try and direct events from the side-lines with humans as pawns. These humans were members of various secret societies that purported to have secret hidden information that would give the members the ability to rule over their neighbors.

Secret societies have been with us since the beginning of recorded history, after all everyone likes to know a secret that he thinks his friends do not know. I am sure that each one of us knows or has known someone who is a member of a secret society. Membership in these types of organizations is usually viewed as a harmless distraction for men and women to take part in as an amusement. However, this is actually the furtherest thing from the truth. Secret Societies are neither for amusement nor a mere distraction, in fact they are, or can be, the worst threats to freedom that exist.

ON THE TRAIL

To study something, you have to at least know what the focus of your study is called. Unfortunately with the Eternal Conspiracy, it has been called many things by many people. This organization has been called "The Insiders", the "Great Conspiracy", the "Illuminati" and hundreds of other names. I believe that all of these names identify the same basic group of people. The Conspiracy seems to take a different name each time it raises its' ugly head. Then if it is defeated, it goes underground until next time it decides it is time to strike.

Mankind, after an unbelievable loss of life in putting down the threat posed by the Conspiracy, believing that the danger is past, the evil is dead, then becomes careless and the Conspiracy strikes again. Unfortunately, while millions have died on both sides of this "hidden" war the Conspiracy itself never seems to die.

But let us look at some descriptions of what we purpose to study. What is this Conspiracy? The following excerpts are from various writers who have either studied the secret societies or been prominent members in them.

> *"Beneath the broad tide of human history there flows the stealthy undercurrents of the secret societies, which frequently determine in the depths, the changes that take place upon the surface[52]."*
>
> *". . .there is a power so organized, so subtle, so complete, so pervasive, that they had better not speak above their breath when they speak in condemnation of it.[53]"*
>
> *"All secret societies and associations-. had two doctrines, one concealed and reserved for the Masters, .the other public. .[54]"*

---

[52] Waite, Arthur Edward, THE REAL HISTORY OF THE ROSICRUCIANS, Steinerbooks, Blauvelt, N.Y. 1977.
[53] Sutton, Antony C., AMERICA'S SECRET ESTABLISHMENT, Liberty House Press, 2027 Iris, Billings, Montana 59102. 1986.
[54] Pike, Albert, MORALS AND DOGMA, The Supreme Council of the Southern Jurisdiction of the Scottish Rite. 1871.

"I don't believe in great providential men, political celebrities owed their reputations, if not to chance, at least to circumstances which they themselves could not have foreseen[55]"

"Not my talents and capacities made me great. But the fact that my mother was the Mistress of Soult, one of the "300", who all helped me.[56]"

"I think there is an elite in this country and they are the ones who run an elitist government. They want a government by a handful of people because they don't believe the people themselves can run their lives. . [57]"

Most researchers believe that all secret societies sprang from the same original secret society. An original secret society that had as its goal, world domination and control. Such a theory would be in keeping with one of the tenets of my theory as follows:

In keeping with my theory, outlined in chapter One, suppose that the original human rulers (The Priest Kings) appointed by the "Gods" (remember, I believe that the "Gods" of ancient history were simply a more advanced race that came to colonize and exploit the earth.) either lost their

---

[55] Quotation from writings of Bismark
[56] Ibid
[57] Quotation from speech by President Ronald Reagan.

power or were simply unable to maintain charismatic control when the "Gods" were forced to distance themselves from mankind. As a result, these "Servants of the Gods" who were ruling mankind were reduced to being religious leaders as they tried to keep control of men's minds once they lost control of men's bodies.

As civilization became more settled, so to speak, stronger, more charismatic leaders took the place of the Priest Kings as secular head or King. Since the Priest Kings could no longer directly rule as Kings, these religious leaders worked behind the scenes to take control of the governments by controlling the ruling King. There are many examples of this program being effective, ancient Egypt is a prime example.

Usually, this control was taken through the utilization of secret societies that included as members, many highly placed members of the government. The reward promised these government officials for betraying their King, or Pharaoh as it was in Egypt, was usually the promise of riches and power on earth and then, since they were usually told it was their god's will that this betrayal take place, guaranteed admittance to heaven or whatever their hereafter was called.

This program of control behind the scenes was first instituted in ancient Sumeria, the first recorded civilization.

As time progressed, there were differences of opinion among the human members of this first secret society and various splinter groups were begun that in time, became competitors with the original conspiracy. Each splinter group was headed by a charismatic leader who purported to speak with the "Gods" and to know the true plan of the "Gods".

At one time, there are so many different secret societies that it is hard to tell one from another. For example, most

Figure 4: George Washington

people think that Adam Weishaupt's Illuminati was the most evil organization that ever lived. However, most tend to overlook the fact that Adam Weishaupt's Illuminati did not openly exist for very many years before the Bavarian authorities suppressed it. However, it is alleged that Weishaupt received his training from another secret society, or secret order, if you will, the Jesuits. Additionally, it is entirely possible that his Order of Illuminated Ones, which was only formed in 1776, and allegedly suppressed in the 1780's, was a blind for the real Illuminated Ones, the

Annanaki.

Figure 5: Adam Weishaupt

(Author's Note: There is a legend that George Washington and Adam Weishaupt looked remarkably alike and that after the suppression of his order in the 1780's, Weishaupt came to the United States, killed George Washington and took his place. It is true that many of Washington's policies as President had a striking similarity with those of Weishaupt.)

If this is true, as many suspect, that Weishaupt's organization was a cover for the "real" Illuminated Ones, then it is these real Illuminati that directed the activities of the organization founded by Adam Weishaupt. These controllers do the dirty work and Weishaupt's dupes get the blame. It would not be the first time that this has happened.

THE REAL POWERS THAT BE

It is also amazing that most "normal" humans tend to overlook the real power of these secret orders. It seems that these secret orders are the real powers on this earth. Almost every nation has had to deal with the power of these orders. The French Revolution seems to be an example of what happens when these Secret Orders get the upper hand.

It is also very revealing that even some of the most famous names in world history believed in a behind the scenes secret order. Consider, if you will, the quotation from Bismark earlier in this chapter, where he talked about French Marshall Soult being a member of the "300". This "300" was, and probably still is, a European organization whose membership is secret. This organization is allegedly the High Government of the Jewish Race, founded by Theodor Herzl, the founder of modern Zionism[58].

Consider the writings of Mr. Manly P. Hall, a famous Masonic writer. It was Mr. Hall who wrote:

> *"[they]. . .are the invisible powers behind the thrones of earth, and men are but marionettes, dancing while the invisible ones pull the strings. We see the dancer, but the master mind that does the work remains concealed by the cloak of silence.[59]"*

In the same work Mr. Hall, incidentally, a 33rd degree Mason, also wrote:

---

[58] Nocolov, Nicola, THE WORLD CONSPIRACY, TOPS, 10170 S.W. Nimbus, Portland, OR 97223.
[59] Hall, Manley P., What The Ancient Wisdom Expects Of Its Disciples, The Philosophical Research Society, Inc. L.A. 1982.>

"In the remote past the gods walked with men and . . .they chose from among the sons of men the wisest and the truest.

With these specially ordained and illumined sons they left the keys of their great wisdom, which was the knowledge of good and evil.

. . .these illumined ones, founded what we know as the Ancient Mysteries[60]."

It would seem that these "Illumined Ones" are the real powers behind the thrones of the earth. So the question must be, how does one become one of these "Illumined Ones"? Mr. Hall also answers this in his book, *THE SECRET TEACHINGS OF ALL AGES.* In this work, he wrote:

"The arcana (or hidden knowledge) of the ancient Mysteries were never revealed to the profane (someone who is not one of the insiders) except through the media of symbols. Symbolism fulfilled the dual office of concealing the sacred truths from the uninitiated and revealing to those qualified to understand the symbols[61]."

So consider what we have found. There is a body of

---

[60] Ibid
[61] Hall, Manley P., THE SECRET TEACHINGS OF ALL AGES, The Philosophical Research Society, Inc. L.A. 1977.

knowledge that is known to only a few chosen Illumined Ones. Using this knowledge, the Illumined Ones control all of the thrones of the earth. It also appears that through the various secret societies, this information is passed to new Illumined Ones, carefully selected by those already possessing the information. Interesting concept. Is this how the Annanaki, or the Ancient Gods, control human affairs?

So what are these Ancient Mysteries? I would give you a clue to what one of the supposedly most learned segments of our human society thinks of these Ancient Mysteries in pointing out that almost every established religion has tried to stamp out the secret societies and with the societies, the Ancient Mysteries. For example, it used to be forbidden for a Catholic to become a Mason. Why?

We appear to get the answer from the writings of Mr. Albert G. Mackey in his two volume work, **ENCYCLOPEDIA OF FREEMASONRY**. Mr. Mackey, also a 33rd degree Mason, was considered by many researchers to be the foremost and most accurate of the Masonic writers. He wrote:

"Each of the pagan gods. . .had, besides the public and open, a secret worship paid to him to which none were admitted but those who had been selected by preparatory ceremonies called Initiation.

This secret worship was termed the Mysteries[62]."

Also, in his **ENCYCLOPEDIA OF FREEMASONRY**, Mr. Mackey also wrote that Adam Weishaupt (alleged founder of the Illuminati) was a radical in politics and an infidel in religion, and that he organized the Illuminati, not more for the purpose of aggrandizing himself, **than of overturning Christianity and the institutions of society[63]**.

Henri Martin, the famed French historian wrote in his **HISTOIRE DE FRANCE**, that "Weishaupt had made into an absolute theory the misanthropic gibes of Rousseau at the invention of property and society, and . . . he proposed as the end of Illuminism the abolition of property, social authority and nationality. . ."

I would observe that the ideas of Weishaupt sound suspiciously like those of the Karl Marx and the Communist Party, coincidence?

So there we have it, the Ancient Mysteries was, and probably still is, a body of knowledge that was feared by organized religion. It is also that body of knowledge that allows the Illumined Ones to control the thrones of earth. Much that has been written about these Ancient Mysteries

---

[62] Mackey, Albert G., AN ENCYCLOPEDIA OF FREEMASONRY, The Masonic History Company, New York. 1873.
[63] Ibid

makes it seem that these Mysteries appear to actually be knowledge of and a secret worship of the pagan gods.

To take this proposal a step further, my theory supposes that the so-called pagan gods were actually real living advanced beings that colonized this planet from elsewhere in the solar system. The alleged Ancient Mysteries is secret knowledge that is actually training and teaching from these advanced beings so that their protégés can control their fellow men.

THE TRUE ADEPT

According to Manly Hall, the true Adept revealed his identity to no one, unless that person was worthy of having that information. But it is believed that these Adepts had the knowledge to solve humanities problems. It is presupposed that what Mr. Hall calls a true Adept is actually an Illumined One.

Mr. Hall further wrote:

". . .no reasonable doubt can exist that the initiates of Greece, Egypt and other ancient countries possessed the correct solutions to those great cultural, intellectual, moral and social problems which in an unsolved state confront the

humanity of the twentieth century[64].

So it is entirely possible that you may know a true adept, but since he never reveals himself, you look at him as just one of the crowd. This means that there are among us individuals who have the answer to the problems that are plaguing mankind, but they refuse to reveal this information. However, ask yourself, what is a true adept? On the one hand the true adept can be someone who was trained in the teachings of the Annanaki or, it is quite possible, the true adept can actually be one of the Annanaki, whose true identity is concealed so that he, or she, can walk among us ordinary mortals.

I would point out that many U.F.O. abductees have talked about agents of the so-called "aliens" walking among us as they carry out their masters' bidding. The stories of the mysterious "Men-in-Black" are to be found in the history of almost every race on this planet.

WHAT'S IT ALL ABOUT?

Why do these secret societies and these adepts exist? What is their purpose in working behind the scenes? Why have they caused so much death and destruction in just the

---

[64] Hall, Manley P., THE SECRET TEACHINGS OF ALL AGES, The Philosophical Research Society, Inc. L.A. 1977.

last three hundred years? To answer the questions, the works of several authors, who were allegedly members of this secret movement, must be consulted, as well as the recorded statements of some of the purported leaders of the movement. According to all of these individuals and their written and spoken words, the true purpose toward which these secret orders have been moving is the creation of a **NEW WORLD ORDER**. A **NEW WORLD ORDER** which treats the common man as cattle and puts the control of all resources in the hands of a few. A government by the Elite, or perhaps a long looked for return of the "Gods". Remember that every organized religion talks of the day when "God" returns to rule his creation. Let's look at what some of these New World Order members have had to say:

Associated Press Dispatch-July 26, 1968:
"New York Governor Nelson A. Rockefeller says as President he would work toward international creation of "a new world order'..."

The Declaration of Interdependence-January 30, 1976. (Signed by 32 Senators and 92 Representatives):
"Two centuries ago our forefathers brought forth a new nation; now we must join with others to bring forth a new

world order."

The Seattle Post-Intelligence-April 18, 1975 (A quote by Henry Kissinger):
"Our nation is uniquely endowed to play a creative and decisive role in the new order which is taking form around us."

The Commencement Address at Texas A&M University-May 12, 1989 (From the speech given by President George Bush):
"Ultimately, our objective is to welcome the Soviet Union back into the world order. Perhaps the world order of the future will truly be a family of nations."

To recap at this point, we have some disturbing statements coming from our leaders. People who we have elected, or been appointed by those that we have elected, are actually proposing something that may not be in our best interest. We see Gov. Nelson Rockefeller, who later became vice-president under President Ford, vowing to work for a "new world order." Then we have large portion of the elected Congress signing a declaration proposing to work for a "new world order."

Henry Kissinger is well known for his involvement with the Rockefeller faction, so his desire for a "new world order" is no surprise. However, it is all together a different thing to have former President, George H. W. Bush reference the new world order as an accomplished fact. It makes one wonder and fear for the safety of our country. It seems that we are surrounded by traitors. In later chapters, we will look closer at both Mr. Rockefeller and Mr. Kissinger.

But these statements really should not be any great surprise when everyone of the above referenced people, to include our current President are avowed members of the Council on Foreign Relation (CFR) a "public" secret society whose charter calls for the creation of a "one world government."

LOOKING BACK

However, the new world order adherents in our so-called freely elected government are nothing new. One important example comes from World War I. Our President at this time was Woodrow Wilson, a man who campaigned on a promise to keep us out of the war. In actuality a good, honest man who strongly believed in this country and the American people believed in him and put him into office.

Unfortunately, immediately after the election,

President Wilson's closest friend, closest Presidential advisor and a man who, by many, was called the President's "alter ego" Colonel Edward Mandell House [the Colonel was honorary] began to work behind the scenes to force our entry into the war brewing in Europe.

I would submit that the actions of Colonel House show that Woodrow Wilson planned all along to get this country into the "Great War". Without the President's knowledge and approval, it would have been impossible for Colonel House to manipulate people and events as history shows that he did.

How could a mere Presidential Advisor act with such independent power and authority? Even more importantly, why would this little known member of the Wilson Administration want us to get into the War? We will examine the background of this mysterious individual in a later chapter, but suffice it to say that his first loyalty was not to the United States, even though he was a close friend and an advisor to the President. To get an insight into the motivations of Colonel House, let's look at what Historian Walter Mills had to say about him.

> "The Colonel's sole justification for preparing such a batch of blood for his countrymen was his hope of establishing a new world order of peace and security."

So the Colonel, based on his "hope for peace and security" was instrumental in getting us into a long, costly and bloody war. A European War that was actually a family argument between related monarchs. This was only one of series of Wars that had erupted in Europe since the Middle Ages. Had the U.S. not intervened, the war would have ended with the establishment of a new balance of power, but the stability of Europe would have remained as would the royal families who had ruled over their various countries for centuries.

World War I was a war that set the stage for World War II and the changing of our world forever. An unelected official having this kind of power should be unthinkable. But in a later chapter you will see much more of Colonel House and his "surprising friends".

So in this chapter, we have begun to get an insight into the Conspiracy and some of the people who have been members. Remember, this Conspiracy is not a thing of the past to be studied dispassionately, but it is alive, well and living among us today, being controlled from the shadows by a faceless cabal.

However, you have no real idea of what this Conspiracy is capable of today until you look at some of the things that its members have been responsible for in the past. The members of this Conspiracy are not radicals hiding in some back room and plotting the downfall of the nation against fantastic odds. On the contrary, the members of this Conspiracy occupy some of the most power positions in this land. The question is, who do they answer to, certainly not the American people.

After having said all of the preceding, in the next chapter we will look at the possibility that elected governments not withstanding that there is an organization that crosses international borders and insures behind the scenes cooperation between outwardly hostile parties.

CHAPTER FIVE

WE HAVE MET THE ENEMY AND HE IS US

Lies! Lies! It cannot be! The wars we wage are noble, and our battles are won by Justice for us, ere we lift the gage. We have not sold our loftiest heritage. The proud republic hath not stooped to cheat and scramble in the marketplace of war; Her forehead weareth yet its solemn star. . . . Was it for this our fathers kept the law?   William Vaughn Moody

Many of you are of the great school of thought that says, history is dead and what happened then can't bother us now. Well, I propose to show you that you are wrong. I propose to prove to you that the Conspiracy of which I write is alive and well and living in America. I have made allegations that members of this hidden Conspiracy occupy positions within our government. Am I just rambling or can I back up what I say? You have to be the judge, but I would ask you to withhold making decisions until after you have completed this volume. Perhaps what I report is coincidence, perhaps simply bad judgment on the part of U.S. Officials; perhaps I am paranoid or reading too much into otherwise innocent actions. However, remember the **James Bond School of Thought:**

- *Once is happenstance*
- *Twice is coincidence, but*
- *Three times is enemy action.*

Based upon the actions of our State Department, I would say that we have found enemy action. However, I offer the evidence in order for you to be the judge.

THE FIRST STEP

As a first step in examining this hidden conspiracy, I am going to show you some of what is happening today. I am going to take you behind the scenes of some of the so-called State Department errors, and some of the so-called coups, that commentators have talked about since World War II. Once we are finished, see if you think that these were actual errors, after all.

The main idea to keep in mind is that each of the so-called errors was the handiwork of State Department officials that were primarily members of the Council on Foreign Relations (CFR) and were, for the most part, all trained in the Ivy League Schools. Later we will see why this last characteristic might be important.

A JUST WAR IS A GOOD WAR

We like to think that all our wars are just. That we fight for Truth, Justice and the American way. Since the late 1940's our enemy has been the "Evil Empire" of the Soviet Union. In the many "brushfire" wars and "police actions" thousands of American soldiers and untold millions of civilian "innocent bystanders" have died under the tank threads of the Russian Army, either directly or indirectly through Soviet controlled "freedom fighters". The Russian Army that we, allegedly, proudly stand ready to combat, outnumbered that we are. It is also to our everlasting shame, an Army that we bought and paid for with American dollars and American technology.

I can hear you all right now. "IMPOSSIBLE!" you say. We would never help the Godless Communists. We are the last bastion of freedom in this old world. Right---and I have a bridge I want to sell you.

We spend billions of dollars for defense every year against an enemy that we armed and trained. An enemy that we re-arm and retrain every year. Confused? Well you are not alone.

DEFENSELESS WE STAND

It may surprise you to know that in spite of all the nuclear missiles that this country is alleged to control, that we are virtually defenseless to a Russian attack. That's right, I said that we are virtually defenseless to an attack by the Russians or anyone else for that matter.

Our nuclear arsenal is an offensive weapon, not defensive. Our arsenal is designed to destroy the enemy in his homeland, not defend our own homes. To defend our homes, we have to depend on the standing military. A military that our Congress is in the process of trying to reduce in size due to the "outbreak of peace." (However, as I write this we have just finished ten years of war and are now facing a new threat) we are calling up our reserves for our newest "moral war" in the Middle East, but more on this in a later chapter. While at the same time, we are happily sending money to our new friends in the Soviet Bloc that is being used to strengthen their armies.

So what keeps the Russians from attacking this country? Their army is bigger and better armed than our own. Their armored vehicles are bigger and more powerful than our own. The Soviet air force and navy out number ours considerably. So what is our defense? According to our government, our best defense is their knowledge that if they destroy us, we destroy them, or the concept of Mutually Assured Destruction.

MUTUAL ASSURED DESTRUCTION

The concept of mutual assured destruction or MAD was designed or the phrase was coined back in the 1960's. At this time, if you will remember, it was expected that the Russians would attack just anytime. Billions went into defense against an enemy who was almost a match for us militarily. An enemy that in 1945 had a shattered economic base, literally millions of casualties from World War II and no international military force to speak of.

On the other hand, we had the atomic bomb, the most powerful military in the world, a navy that could sweep any other country from the seas and an air force second to none. We had the power to literally destroy any country that we chose. In our magnanimous way, we set out the rebuild the world in our image. But something went wrong. Something went very badly wrong.

In less than twenty years or less than one generation, Russia went from a second rate power to one that has eclipsed us in military power. It has nuclear weapons to match or outclasses our own, a military that is second to none, aircraft that can outclass our own and a navy that out numbers ours. How could this happen? Wouldn't the cost of such a military machine mean that the common people would starve, that the economy would be in a shambles?

At the same time that the Soviet Military Machine has been building, we have been disarming as fast as we can go. We have rifted, or fired, many of our finest, combat trained military officers, moth balled our mighty fleet and allowed what we didn't retire to become outdated and refused to replace our strategic air force. We know that the Soviet Union out numbers us in Intercontinental Ballistic Missiles (ICBM) but we have no anti-ballistic missile system (ABM). The most unnerving part of this is that this lack of a competent ABM system is by agreement with the Soviet Union. In other words, we agreed to disarm ourselves[65].

According to the concept of mutually assured destruction, neither we nor the Soviets are supposed to have a defensive capability, only offensive. In other words, what would keep us from starting a war would be the certain knowledge that we would also be destroyed. Of course, such a concept was tailor made for the liberal media that has always viewed Russia as heaven on earth. Our own media has implied that we would be the ones to start the war, not the

---

[65] Bearden, T. E., <u>FER DE LANCE</u>, Tesla Book Co. Greenville, TX 75401. 1986.

Soviets. Interesting concept.

WE HAVE THE BEST ENEMY THAT MONEY CAN BUY

As pointed out by Antony C. Sutton in his book, *The Best Enemy Money Can Buy*[66], the United States has been the greatest aid that the Soviet Union could ever have had in its military aims. Before all of you liberals start howling about my casting aspersions on the greatest man in history (some have even rated him a step above Jesus Christ) Michael Gorbachev, let me offer some examples:

In December, 1979, the Soviet Union invaded Afghanistan (It should be remembered that our President, Jimmy "Mr. Peanut" Carter "got tough with Moscow" in response to the invasion. He withheld our Olympic Team from the Moscow Olympics. Can you picture the hardship that this caused the Soviet leadership?).

The initial Soviet forces flew into Afghanistan on what were supposed to be civilian flights. Once on the ground at the main airport in Kabul, they quickly seized control of the city. The operation worked smoothly for these flights were filled with the cream of the Soviet Army, the

---

[66] Sutton, Antony C., THE BEST ENEMY MONEY CAN BUY, Liberty House Press. Billings. Montana. 1986.

Soviet Special Forces. However, the main forces, especially the armored columns, came overland, by road.

The Soviet Army mounted a massive invasion of a country surrounded by some of the most impassable mountains in the world. How did the soviets get their armored columns and especially their massive main battle tanks to such a backward, mountainous country? Why over a road built courtesy of the United States Government.

This road building project was begun at the order of President Lyndon Baines Johnson as part of his "Great Society"[67]. At a time when the United States was in need of funds for numerous social programs for our own citizens, and when funds were needed to support our troops fighting in the midst of the Vietnam War. At a time when thousands of our troops were being killed by weapons sent to North Vietnam from the Soviet Union, President Johnson sent U.S. Engineers to work with the Soviets to build, what amounted to, two super highways from the Soviet Union to Kabul.

It is interesting to note that two wide, modern highways had to be built. Due to the mountainous terrain, each of the highways had to have several reinforced bridges constructed. In a country where the heaviest vehicle might be an old pickup truck, these highways have bridges specifically

---

[67] Ibid

designed to be capable of holding thirty (30) ton Soviet tanks. To build this road cost the American Taxpayers more than $640,000 per mile. What is the purpose of building such roads going to so desolate a place, except military traffic?

A HIGHER REALITY

The following is an excerpt from a speech given by the Russian Revolutionary Vladimir Ilych (Ulyanov) Lenin

"The Capitalists of the world and their governments, in pursuit of conquest of the Soviet market, will close their eyes to the indicated higher reality and thus will turn into deaf mute blind men. They will extend credits, which will strengthen for us *the Communist Party in their countries and giving us the materials and technology we lack, they will restore our military industry, indispensable for our future victorious attacks on our suppliers. In other words, they will labor for the preparation for their own suicide.*[68]*"*

This "Higher Reality" represents Lenin's belief that Communism is the final fate of the world and only the capitalists fail to realize this. He felt, apparently rightly, that capitalism as a system would be responsible for its own downfall. In a system where everything is for sale, the system

---

[68] Finder, Joseph, <u>RED CARPET</u>, Holt, Rinehart & Winston, New York. 1984.

would sell itself if the money was right.

The idea of higher reality has not been a secret; in fact the Soviets have told anyone who would listen. The Communists have talked about it for years, only most Americans have never heard of it. The reason for this ignorance is quite simple; our own government covered this up. The leaders responsible for seeing that our system survived, have been hiding the fact our government has been selling our enemies the very things that they need to defeat us.

I'M FROM THE GOVERNMENT, TRUST ME!

A prime example of this was some of the acts of the U.S. State Department under Secretary of State John Foster Dulles. Secretary of State Dulles appointed Dr. G. Bernard Noble as head of the Historical Office of the State Department. This office was, and is, responsible for keeping historical records regarding State Department functions and programs. However, it is alleged that under Dr. Noble, there was an official policy of distorting information and suppressing historical documents. It should be noted that Dr. Noble was a Rhodes Scholar, a designation which as you shall see later, makes him suspect.

There were two other historians, Dr. Donald Dozer

and Dr. Bryton Barron, who were also working in the State Department at this time. Both made the mistake of protesting this policy of information suppression and distortion. As is usually the case in government jobs, the powers that be decided that they were not "team players", so they were both terminated.

Dr. Barron later wrote a book on his experiences, called *Inside the State Department*[69]. In this book, he made some very serious charges regarding what he termed high level wrong doing. This high level wrong doing would be called treason by some.

Dr. Barron specifically charged that officials in our State Department were directly responsible for exporting military technology to the Soviet Union. Among the examples he discussed were:

- Equipment designed specifically for manufacturing jet engines.
- Boring mills used in manufacturing tanks, artillery, aircraft and submarine atomic reactors.
- Equipment used to balance shafts on engines for jets and guided missiles.
- Grinding machines essential in making engine parts,

---

[69] Barron, Bryton, INSIDE THE STATE DEPARTMENT, Comet Press, New York. 1956.

guided missiles and radar.

So as you can see, not only does the State Department arm our enemies, but anyone who would alert the citizens of this nation to the betrayal and treason being carried out by the State Department is fired. All in the name of National Security, of course.

THE COVER-UP

In order to cover-up the fact the Russian scientific advances are nothing more than "copying" of our technology, our own State Department has created the myth of the Soviet "genius". According to reports coming out of our State Department, the Soviet scientific community is making massive strides forward in developing modern technology. Yet, the State Department's own historical records show massive U.S. assistance since the 1917 Revolution.

To show examples of the on-going continuing cover-up, consider the following:

November 28, 1917, just after the Bolsheviks overthrew the Russian government, "Colonel" E.M. House, President Woodrow Wilson's alter ego and closest advisor wired the President and the Secretary of State the following cable from Paris[70].

There has been cabled over and published here statements made by American papers to the effect that Russia should be treated as an enemy. It is exceedingly important that such criticisms should be suppressed.

As a result of this cable, the statements referred to above were stopped. It seems that "Colonel" House had a great deal of power in the Wilson administration. But we shall see a great deal more of "Colonel" House as we progress through this sordid tale of betrayal and treason.

In 1968, the following statement was attributed to Nicholas de B. Katzenbach, (a C.F.R. member) then Assistant Secretary of State.

"We should give no illusions. If we do not sell peaceful goods to the nations of Eastern Europe, others will. If we erect barriers to our trade with Eastern Europe, we will lose the trade and Eastern Europe will buy elsewhere. But we will not make any easier our task of stopping aggression in Vietnam nor in building security for the United States[71].

However, facts show that much of the technology

---

[70] Sutton, Antony C., THE BEST ENEMY MONEY CAN BUY, Liberty House Press. Billings, Montana. 1986.
[71] Ibid

used by the Soviets to build the military equipment that they exported to North Vietnam came from the United States. However, the State Department's idea of peaceful goods leaves something to be desired. To get a good idea of the "changing nature of peaceful goods", we need to go back to 1945 and the end of World War II.

The victorious Allies had to decide what to do with a defeated Germany. The U.S. Government set up a special commission to determine what should be done with the German automobile industry. This special committee concluded that any motor vehicle industry in any country is an important aspect of that country's war potential. The following were the findings of the committee:

- Any motor vehicle industry is a major factor in a country's war making capability.
- German automotive manufacturing should be prohibited because it was a war industry.
- Numerous military products can be made by the automobile industry. The committee attached a list containing over 300 items with strictly military applications[72].

---

[72] STUDY BY INTERAGENCY COMMITTEE ON THE TREATMENT OF THE GERMAN AUTOMOTIVE INDUSTRY FROM THE STANDPOINT OF NATIONAL SECURITY.

HAVE A NICE GORBAZAM

Now re-read the above carefully. Look at number 2 above: German automotive manufacturing should be prohibited because it was a war industry. Now I ask you, if automotive manufacturing is a war industry for Germany, wouldn't logic dictate that automotive manufacturing would be a war industry for Soviet Russia?

Surprisingly, in a similar study, some of the same committee members decided that automotive manufacturing would not be a war industry in Russia. Even more surprising, this decision was made with the members of this second committee being fully aware of the Soviet's officially intention (Stated as early as 1927) to use foreign automobile technology for military vehicles.

As if this official stated position wasn't enough, V.V. Ossinsky, one of the Soviet Army's top planners wrote several articles for Pravda in 1927 that discussed the use of such automobile technology for military purposes. The entire current Soviet military-civilian manufacturing industry is made up of a few large plants designed, built by and equipped with American technology. Current estimates reveal that about 90-95% of Soviet military vehicles are built

---

(Washington D.C.: Foreign Economic Administration, July 14, 1945), Report T.I.D.C. No. 12.

in plants designed by American Engineers and built by American companies. Among these American companies are such giants as:

- Ford Motor Company
- A.J. Brandt Company
- Austin Company
- General Electric
- Swindell-Dressler
- Budd
- Hamilton Foundry[73]

Now I ask you, why the double standard? Why was it decided that Germany couldn't have an automotive manufacturing capability, but Soviet Russia could? Why did the U.S. Government *give* One Billion ($1,000,000,000.00) dollars to build the largest truck manufacturing plant in the world in Soviet Russia? (It covers 36 acres and produces more military trucks than the entire U.S. output combined.)[74]

Could there be forces behind the scenes that we have no idea exist? Could these forces be manipulating our government like a puppet on a string?

The answers to all these questions will become evident as we progress. Suffice it say at this point that *there is a secret*

---

[73] Sutton, Antony C., THE BEST ENEMY MONEY CAN BUY. Liberty House Press. Billings, Montana. 1986.
[74] Ibid

society controlling our government and most of the Governments of the world. Doubt me? The proof will be shown as you progress.

TWENTY FIRST CENTURY WEAPONS

While we have been happily helping arm the Soviet Army, our scientific establishment has been helping modernize other areas of the Soviet Empire. In fact, some of the Soviet's most advanced work has been based on research done in the United States and passed onto Soviet officials.

One example has been work in the field of Scalar Electromagnetics[75]. This field is an extension of present electromagnetics to include the force known as gravitation. This field was originally developed by Nikola Tesla, one of the most brilliant individuals in history.

Through the use of scalar electromagnetics, electromagnetic field energy can be turned into gravitational field energy and vice versa. Using writing published in American literature, Soviet researchers have developed a method of using this field as a weapon.

Using this continuing research, the Soviets have launched the largest most expensive weapons research

---

[75] Bearden, T. E., FER DE LANCE, Tesla Book Co. Greenville, TX 75401. 1986.

program in history. More importantly, they have kept it hidden from prying eyes. These new weapons are now deployed and have been tested several times. We have turned a blind eye to the entire program, even when one of their tests resulted in the deaths of Americans, on national television.

ENERGETICS[76]

The Soviets call this type of advanced weapons science energetics. We have believed that this term is only associated with; conventional directed energy weapons such as the legendary particle beam weapon, lasers and such. All of which were based on American research and discoveries which were given to the Soviets.

As early as 1960, then Premier, Nikita Khrushchev, announced that the Soviets had a fantastic new weapon. On May 1, 1960, the U-2 spy plane of Francis Gary Powers was brought down by this new weapon. It is alleged that on April 10, 1963, one of the new weapons based on this research destroyed the U.S.S. Thresher, one of our atomic subs.

In Vietnam, some of our F-111's were brought down with some type of energy beam which caused the emergency indicator lamps to light up like Christmas trees. In fact, the Vietnam conflict was used as a testing ground for many

---

[76] Ibid

Soviet developed weapons systems. All of which were based on American research.

So we must face the facts that our government has helped the communists create their movement, consolidate their power, conquer free countries all over the globe, build up their military and advance their scientific establishment. As we shall later see, moneyed interests in this country have also helped fund the communists. At the same time, we spend billions to defend ourselves from these same forces.

Now comes the most important questions of all:

1. *Why would government officials in our own government be willing to work for the downfall of our government?*

Could the answer to this question be that perhaps these government officials owe their first loyalty to some organization other than the U.S. government?

2. *Why would the most powerful capitalists in the world be willing to not only help the communists create their government (a government dedicated to destroying the capitalistic system) but also to fund said government when it couldn't even feed its' own people?*

Could it be that in some way those aforesaid capitalists actually have some control over the communist movement?

Assuming that the most powerful capitalists in the world are not stupid, then they would only act out of self-interest. Why would supporting the communists be in the best interests of such families as the Rockefellers, Warburgs and the Schiffs? Could they either know something that we don't, or are they much more involved in the interworkings of the Soviet Union than they would want us to know? Could these powerful families be involved in the Conspiracy? Let us look further.

CHAPTER SIX

THE OCCULT PATH

The world is governed by very different personages from what is imagined by those who are not behind the scenes. Benjamin Disraeli

Most people, if they consider the issue at all, seem to believe that the word "Occult" has something to do with Satan worship and the forces of darkness. As a result, many would-be researchers into the Occult world have been forced to end their studies due to the pressure from religious and other well-meaning groups. The religious groups seem to feel that if someone wishes to study occult matters then he must be inherently evil. Such an attitude is equivalent to "Ignore it and it will go away." In other words, if no one studies the occult, then there will be much less evil in the world. Unfortunately this is not the case, for I would submit that if one is not inherently evil, merely studying a subject will not make the student evil and all of the bible study in the world would not make a would-be Hitler a minister.

On the other hand, a materialist individual dismisses the occult as just so much hocus pocus. Obviously, a person who studies the occult is someone who deals with fantasy and as a direct result, is not someone who will be successful in this materialistic world. (Add to this that it is the materialistic individual who usually rises to positions of power and importance and it is easy to see how THE CONSPIRACY has lasted as long as it has.) Therefore, it comes as a great surprise to learn that some of the most famous people in history were very much involved in occult matters and steeped in occult knowledge. It is a further shock to the materialistic point of view that many major historical events in our history have hidden meanings that can only be interpreted through an understanding of occult lore.

Before we delve into the world of the strange and bizarre, I think that a general knowledge of certain topics is required. The first step in understanding occult lore is knowing what the word occult actually means. Our religious leaders, with the help of the CONSPIRACY, itself, have endeavored to equate occult with Satanic. Nothing could be further from the truth. The word occult simply means "hidden"[77]. The occult path is quite simply, the hidden path. It is to this hidden path that we must go in order to find out for ourselves what is really happening in our world.

Why do men seek out the hidden path? Why do they dedicate lifetimes and fortunes to the effort of seeking out what is hidden, often with good reason, from men? What can be so attractive that men will brave the unknown and risk everything they have, to achieve it? Quite simply, it is POWER- whether it be over nature herself or other men, the goal of those who seek the hidden path is POWER.

To begin to understand what is happening today in the underground conspiracy, it is necessary to seek out the roots of these secret societies that protect and disseminate the occult knowledge. For this reason, before we get down to talking about the present, it is important that we penetrate the mists of time and examine the beginnings of what may be the first secret society on the planet - THE CULT OF ISIS.

THE CULT OF ISIS

Isis was one of the first goddess in the time of pre-history. She was allegedly THE GODDESS from which

---

[77] Howard, Michael, THE OCCULT CONSPIRACY,. Destiny Books, Rochester, Vermont. 1989

all other gods and goddess sprang. But at the same time, she always remained a virgin. There is much speculation that ISIS was the original Mother goddess worshiped by man prior to the other ancient religions beginning.

Figure 6: Egyptian Goddess Isis

According to much research conducted over the last few years, The Cult of Isis was formed to pass on some advanced scientific learning that had to do with the creation of the human race. It is very possible, that in the occult teachings of the Cult of Isis is the very proof of my theory. For you see, Isis was allegedly one of the Annanaki who helped create our race. Most importantly, the answer to this question is within reach, for researchers have pinpointed what may have been the burial place of Isis, herself, (legend says that even the Gods could die under certain circumstances) in France[78].

Isis had a major effect on the human race. Her teachings even pervade most of our modern religions. Most

---

[78] Wood, David, GENISIS, The First Book of Revelations, The Baton Press. Tunbridge Wells, Kent. 1985.

are totally unbelieving when I point out that teachings of the ISIS CULT are to be found in the teachings of Christianity. Researchers far more versed in these matters than I point to several areas of the BIBLE that allegedly describe initiations ceremonies for new members of the ISIS CULT[79].

Perhaps in a later book I will delve into the Isis Cult, but at this time, I have another fish to fry, so to speak. Therefore, let us move onto the three "human" secret organizations that have had an impact on our society:

1.) The Prieure de Sion,

2.) The Order of the Rosy Cross, and

3.) Freemasonry.

FREEMASONRY

Figure 7: Symbol of Freemasonry

Most secret societies have managed to, more or less, remain hidden from public view. Not so, Freemasonry. The Masonic Orders have been very much in the public eye, in almost every country where they exist. It has been much rumored that membership in the

---

[79] Ibid

Masons can be a great assist in climbing up the ladder in the business world, a claim which the Masons, themselves, deny. Many of the Membership claim that the Masons is nothing for than a social organization like the Lions club. Allegedly, it is a group that works to improve the world. Of course, if this is the case, then why do the majority of judges, lawyers, businessmen and military officers maintain membership? However, most fail to realize that Masonry is one of the most important, powerful and influential organizations of modern time.

As Bernard Fay wrote in his book REVOLUTION AND FREEMASONRY, 1680-1800[80]:

"The new faith in the future of humanity that spread in the eighteenth century was not simply an abstract fact or a mental force. It became a social force and a concrete fact through the agency of Freemasonry, which at once accepted it and advocated it; the great historical importance of modern Freemasonry results from this attitude that it took then. . . . Thus Freemasonry has become the most efficient social power of the civilized world. But it has been a hidden power, difficult to trace, to describe and to define. Consequently, most historians have avoided treating it

---

[80] Fay, Bernard, <u>REVOLUTION AND FREEMASONRY, 1680 1800</u>, Boston: Little, Brown and Co. 1935.

seriously and giving it due credit."

Are Masonic Lodges simply social clubs, or are they something more? It is known that it was in the Masonic Lodges of France that the French Revolution began. In fact, according to legend, the Freemasonry Movement was merged, so to speak, with an even older secret order that had as its' goal world revolution.

It is important to note that the French Masons were the core of the revolution. Was this a fluke or was it part of a master plan that could happen again?

Additionally, here are some other questions that you should ponder:

1.) Can Freemasonry be a source of power for members?
2.) Is Freemasonry a threat to the current world order?
3.) Is Freemasonry a force moving for the New World Order that the One World Government forces desires?

In the context of this present book, we will touch upon each of these questions, but you have to wait for a further book in the Occult Connection series for a thorough examination of these topics.

THE ORDER OF THE ROSY CROSS

The Order of the Rosy Cross rivals Freemasonry in age. According to legend, The Order of the Rosy Cross was created by Egyptian Pharaoh Thothmes III. This was the Pharaoh that built the most famous of the Egyptian Temples at Heliopolis, also called the City of the Sun, in the fifteenth century BCE. [The pillars that guarded the entrance of this famous Temple currently stand on the Thames Embankment in London and are called Cleopatra's Needles.][81]

Figure 8: Symbol of the Rosy Cross

According to a pamphlet called Fama Fraternitatis, or *A Discovery of the Fraternity of the Most Laudable Order of the Rosy Cross*, published at Cassel in 1614, the Order of the Rosy Cross began with one Christian Rosenkreutz, born in 1378. As told in the pamphlet, in 1384, Christian

---

[81] Howard, Michael, THE OCCULT CONSPIRACY, Destiny Books. Rochester, Vermont. 1989.

Rosenkreutz and one other left for Damascus, Syria to learn from the masters. His companion died and left Rosenkreutz, a merely youth of about 16 years of age to continue the journey.

In the Far East, Rosenkreutz is alleged to have learned the Jewish Cabala from which he gathered the secrets that are passed down in the Order. Upon his return to Germany, Rosenkreutz gathered around nine brothers who constituted the initiates of his new order. He was the head of this Order until his death in 1484.

In 1604, the, then, inner circle of brothers discovered a heretofore hidden door within their stronghold upon which was written "Post 120 Annos Patebo". Upon opening the door, they discovered a vault which contained a brass tablet. Beneath the brass tablet was the one hundred twenty year old corpse of Christian Rosenkreutz, "whole and unconsumed". In other words, his body had not decayed in over one hundred and twenty years, similar to that of the children who witnessed the Fatima Miracle. Allegedly, much written material was found with the corpse which enlightened the Brotherhood on many matters. One of which was, allegedly, the coming new order in human affairs.

Many believe that Christian Rosenkreutz really lived and did all of the things that legend says that he did. Others believe that the story of this individual is a concoction used to try and give the order an older heritage than it deserves. What is truth, no one knows.

The Order of the Rosy Cross still exists today as an order of learning. Like the Mason's, some look at it with suspicion and some with envy.

THE PRIEURE DE SION

Figure 9: Symbol of the Prieure DE Sion

This Order is one of the most mysterious because even its existence was hidden until recently. According to some researchers, the Prieure de Sion is a very ancient Order that was the inner circle of the Knights Templar, the military monks who kept the Holy Land roads free for travelers. According to legend, this order was a keeper of ancient knowledge and may have had possession or guarded the so called "Holy Grail"[82].

Also according to legend, this Order had the job of

---

[82] Baigent, Michael; Richard Leigh, and Henry Lincoln, HOLY BLOOD, HOLY GRAIL, Dell. New York. 1983.

guarding the descendants and heirs of Christ. There is evidence that the Merovingian Dynasty of France were blood descendants of Christ through his children who were allegedly smuggled out of Palestine. This Order had the job of guarding the blood line[83]. Based in France, this Order exists today and still carries out its ancient task of guarding the pure blood line. According to documents found in Europe, some of the most famous figures of history were members of this Order. The names would shock you.

So now we have discussed four secret societies:

1) The Cult of Isis,
2) The Free Masons,
3) The Order of the Rosy Cross, and
4) The Prieure De Sion.

Of these four which is the one that is today trying to subvert all of our freedoms? The answer will surprise you.

Most who have examined these types of Orders, such as the British Parliament, feel that the Masonic Order is the biggest threat to free government[84]. This in spite of the fact that traditionally, the head of the British Masons has been a

---

[83] Baigent, Michael; Richard Leigh and Henry Lincoln,. THE MESSIANIC LEGACY. Dell. New York. 1986.
[84] Knight, Stephen, THE BROTHERHOOD, The Secret World of the Freemasons, Dorset Press. 1984.

member of the Royal Family.

Such a belief is not without good cause, I might add. There was allegedly a connection between Masonic rituals and the Jack the Ripper Murders in Whitechapel in 1885. There was even a Sherlock Holmes story pointing out that the methods in which the Ripper's victims were mutilated had a great deal in common with the types of injuries suffered by Hiram Abiff, the Architect of the Temple of Solomon in Masonic Lore.

However, there is a great deal of evidence that points to an even more secret society from which all of these stem. This unknown secret society is alleged to have begun untold thousands of years ago and existed under the control of an unbroken chain of masters until the present day. Is this true, or simply the delirious ravings of the worst type of paranoid? Unfortunately in the study of secret organizations it is easy to mistake one of the "fronts" for the actual power behind the scenes. Such an error can result in the cutting off of one head of the Hydra Monster, but still leave the creature living to strike again. Our job is to find the actual "main beast", so to speak. For only in finding and destroying this main beast can we be sure that we have ended the danger once and for all.

A HIDDEN CONNECTION

Before we go on, let's first see if there appear to be any connections between the various sects or movements that we have looked at thus far.

In 1663, there was a Masonic Congress held at which time the first three degrees were created. At this same time, a strong amount of Rosicrucian teaching was introduced into the craft. At this same time, a French Priest named wrote a book wherein he called for the Craft to avenge the Knights Templar, the organization of religious warrior monks had earlier been suppressed by the King of France. Depuis called for the Craft to depose the French King and the Stuart line of England since they were allied with the French Monarchy and most surprising, he also called for the overthrow of the Church, since the Pope had played a hand in the end of the Knights Templar.

From this time forward, a strong faction of the Craft became anti-Stuart, anti-Church and anti-French. Coincidence?

However, an equally large portion of Masonry, called Jacobite Masonry, stayed loyal to the Stuart cause and many even followed deposed Stuart King, James II into exile in France. It was the Jacobite Masons who founded a Catholic lodge at Paris. It was this lodge which eventually became the most militant against the Church and the French Monarchy[85].

In 1717, the Grand Lodge of England was chartered. This became a central authority after a time for lodges in England, part of the Continent and in parts of America. For a determination of what kind of people controlled the Grand Lodge, one must keep in mind that the Grand Lodge was known as an association of Freethinkers. For a better understanding of what constituted being a freethinker, no less a noted writer than Jonathan Swift characterized those called freethinkers as atheists, libertines, and despisers of religion.

It has also been pointed out that the ideology of Masonry, which was characterized by "an indifference to religion and a tendency towards cosmopolitanism and internationalism." This internationalism would supplant the Christian duty of patriotism and loyalty to the State by some kind of ineffective international humanitarianism[86].

Isn't the supplanting of patriotism and loyalty to the State exactly what the Conspiracy is attempting to have happen today, over two hundred years later? Another

---

[85] Kelly, Rev. Clarence, <u>Conspiracy Against God and Man</u>, Western Islands, Belmont, Mass. 1974.
[86] Cahill, E., <u>Freemasonry and the Anti-Christian Movement</u>, M. H. Gill and Son, Ltd., Dublin. 1930.

coincidence?

THE U.F.O. CONNECTION

I am sure at this point, you are asking yourself how this ties in with U.F.O.s and Ancient GODS, since these two topics were also discussed in the first volume of this series. The answer is quite simple. I believe that all three topics are interconnected. The problem is to wade through all of the disinformation and try and get a look at the true picture.

It is my belief that the true goals of all three groups: 1) U.F.O. occupants, 2) Secret Society Members, and 3) The So-Called Ancient Gods were and are in control and have power over this Planet and the Human Race. In the literature, all three have called for a one world order where peace reigns forever, under their control of course. I for one am not in favor of such a happening. I believe that man has a right to arrive at his destiny in his own way and in his own time. We don't need big brother pointing the way.

THE TOPIC

The intent of the entire series is to study the secret societies as far back into history as possible. However, such a study is impossible in a single volume. For this reason, I have chosen to deal with just one area at a time. In this particular volume, I have decided to deal with the most powerful secret societies that have had the most direct impact on our civilization. It may help you understand some of what is going on in the world today. It is all interconnected.

There are many who have theorized that all of the secret societies that inhabit the underground maze of alleged secret knowledge and strange beliefs had their births within the same "family". Even so famous a researcher as Kenneth Mackenzie, himself a Rosicrucian stated in his Masonic Cyclopaedia under the heading "Rosicrucians" that there was a very ancient society which stretched back into the dawn of time from which all of the major secret orders began.

It is my belief that this "very ancient society" has existed since the earliest days of civilization and is still alive and doing well today. I further propose that this "very ancient society" has never made itself known, but has instead acted through other, more public orders. I also believe that it is possible to prove that some of history's most famous, and infamous, have been members of this "very ancient society". In a later chapter, we will discuss some of the "famous" members of this hidden society. Were they working for public good, or working for goals more hidden? Don't rely on my opinion, but, instead, judge for yourself as we delve further into the unknown.

CHAPTER SEVEN

SETTING THE STAGE

There is a power somewhere so organized, so subtle, so watchful, so interlocked, so complete, so pervasive that they better not speak above their breath when they speak in condemnation of it. Woodrow Wilson.

Unfortunately, for the average American Citizen, we are a relatively trusting people. For most of us, paradise would be a refrigerator full of beer and twenty four hour a day football games. We out produce the rest of the world put together, have the highest level of technology the world has ever seen and a form of government that we are willing to die for. Most of us sleep soundly at night knowing that our elected officials are awake watching over us. We are smug in our knowledge that we are the greatest country on earth. I believe that this is true, but I also know that we are living on borrowed time. My research has shown that our governmental mansion has termites. Termites that we put there.

As we begin to examine who, what, when and how, I also want to look at some other beliefs of ours.

1.) Such is our view of the world events that we believe that the American way should be imposed on every other country. We "know" that if we find fault with our government, we can change it without bloodshed. After all, look at Watergate and what happened to Nixon. Proof that our system works. Correct?

2.) Most American pay no attention to government and politics for we feel that our elected representatives know better than we how to do things and after all, we put them there, right?

3.) Americans have always fought on the side of truth and justice. Why look at our history, in the American Revolution we fought against unjust taxes and despotic government.

4.) Unlike most world governments, our government works for the best interests of the American People.

5.) Our elected officials work for the good of the American People.

6.) Our top officials are the most trust worthy people available.

7.) Capitalism is the sworn enemy of Communism, correct?

8.) The world freedom movement of today is proof, positive, that all people want to live free, correct?

If you believe all of the above statements, then I hope that this book will wake you up to the real world. This country has been manipulated, pushed, robbed and generally used since its beginning. The most unfortunate thing is that the culprits have usually been elected officials. The reason for this is that their first loyalty did not lie to this country, but instead to a secret organization that has been working for centuries to control the world and install their favored system of government on the people of the world.

To examine this idea, let's look first at the issues that led up to the American Revolution, circa 1776.

PRELIMINARIES

As I alluded to in the first volume of this series, almost every founding father of this new country was a member of one of the secret societies, but the involvement of secret orders in the forming of the United States is even more pervasive than most realize. Most of these secret societies were naturally European in character. However, what is not generally known is that many of these orders were political in nature. There is a great deal of evidence that many of the European wars were fought in order to advance the philosophy on one or another of these societies.

Another interesting fact about these secret societies is that their plans will span centuries in order to accomplish some goal. Additionally, they will shamelessly use individuals, usually members, but not always so, to accomplish their ends and then abandon these individuals to their own fates once they have accomplished what the Order requires.

In fact, if not for one of these Secret Orders, the Knights Templar, it is possible that Columbus would not have discovered America in 1492[87]. As I have previously mentioned, the Knights Templar were a monastic military

---

[87] Howard, Michael, THE OCCULT CONSPIRACY, Destiny Books. Rochester, Vermont. 1989.

order that was allegedly formed in the Holy Land around 1100 A.D. At one and the same time, there is a great deal known about this legendary band of warriors and little known about them. There is a lot of information known, but the question is how much of it is true? One thing that is true, however, is that this monastic order was actually the first banking order. Money could be deposited at one "Temple" in England and taken out at another "Temple" in France. A concept similar to that used by Banks today.

THE CRUSHING OF THE KNIGHTS TEMPLAR

Figure 10: Flag of the Knights Templar

In the 13th century, around 1307 to be specific, the Knights of the Temple were persecuted by Philippe IV (also called Philippe the Fair) of France and the then reigning Pope. The Knights Templar had become too wealthy and powerful for their own good. On Friday 13, 1307, Philippe caused all Knights Templar within his domains to be arrested and turned over to the Inquisition[88].

---

[88] Baigent, Michael and Richard Leigh, THE TEMPLE AND THE LODGE, Arcade Publishing. New York. 1989.

Even though it was alleged that the Knights had turned from worshiping God to worshiping an idol, the real reason that Philippe crushed the order was to get his greedy hands on the treasures of the Templars.

However, the best laid plans of mice and men often go astray. There is evidence to believe that the Knights knew what was planned for them. Witnesses later testified that the Templar fleet, with many of its knights and the entire treasury set sail shortly before the French raids began. The fleet, the knights on board and the treasure then vanished from the pages of history[89].

It is also known that many Knights, rather than surrender, escaped to other countries where they could hope for sanctuary. Many of these warriors, being considered the best trained fighters in the world, helped change history in their adoptive countries. For example, it was a force of Templars that helped Robert Bruce finally defeats the English in Scotland in 1314. It was actually a very small force of Templars that routed the English Army that day. The mere appearance of a Templar unit on the field was sufficient to send the English forces running. So decisive was the Templar involvement that as a result of their actions,

---

[89] Ibid

Scotland was a free kingdom for the next 289 years[90].

The Order of the Temple, as it was called, had members throughout the then known world. Under the orders of Jacques DeMolay, the last known leader of the Templars, many of the survivors changed the names of their orders. In Portugal, the Knights Templar took the name of the Knights of Christ. It is known, or at least strongly suspected, that Columbus' father-in-law was a member of this Order and it was with charts inherited from this relative that Columbus undertook his voyage[91].

CHRISTOPHER COLUMBUS, INITIATE?

There have been many who have speculated that this was just the first of many occult influences which were involved in making America a super power. There have also been hints that Columbus's association with the Templars may have been much greater than being the son-in-law of a Knight of Christ. In fact, judging by his prominence after his voyages, it would be surprising if Columbus, himself, had not been a member of a secret society.

There have been many historians who assert that Columbus was an illiterate man who was educated by a

---

[90] Ibid
[91] Howard, Michael, THE OCCULT CONSPIRACY, Destiny Books. Rochester, Vermont. 1989.

guild of weavers in Genoa. However, others have pointed out that the guilds were often used as cover by various secret societies who wanted to keep their identities hidden. Unfortunately, this view of Columbus, as an illiterate sailor is not borne out by his writings of later years.

Much about Columbus is legend and rumor. It is known that Columbus had affiliations with supporters of Dante, a former Grand Master of the Order of the Rosy Cross. The romantic story of Isabella of Spain selling her jewelry to finance Columbus's voyages may also be suspect since proof has been found that his voyages of discovery were sponsored by Leonardo da Vinci and Loranzo de Medici, both members of secret societies. These two very influential individuals found Columbus patrons among European Royalty[92].

It is also known that Columbus was very religious, always wearing a brown robe and girdle similar to that worn by Franciscan Monks, and believed that he had a special mission in life. Columbus also heard spirit voices while in trance and believed that the new world was New Jerusalem.

As history reports, later in his life, Columbus was disgraced and returned to Spain in chains only to be restored to favor and allowed one last voyage. His dream of a

---

[92] Ibid

spiritual Utopia on Earth was not to be, as soon after this he died, his dreams seemed to die with him.

SIR FRANCIS BACON

Taking Columbus' place as the torch bearer for the unseen powers in regard to the New world was Sir Francis Bacon (1561-1626). Sir Francis Bacon has been credited with being a genius by many historians. It is even suspected that he was the actual writer of the works of William Shakespeare. What is known is that during his early days as a lawyer, Bacon was initiated into a Secret Society known as the Order of the Helmet. The members of this group worshiped the Greek Goddess of wisdom, Athene (who may also be another name for ISIS). Additionally, Bacon was a student of Hermetic, Gnostic and Neo-Platonist philosophy as well as a student of the Jewish Cabbala[93].

Bacon was also one of those called a Utopian who believed that in some forgotten golden age man lived as one people in peace. He worked for the creation of a future society where all man would live subject to one law and would have no war. (This sounds suspiciously like the "New Order" that the secret societies today work to create.)

Bacon was far more practical than most of the

---

[93] Ibid

Utopians, he created a blueprint for this perceived new order. In 1627, he wrote a novel called THE NEW ATLANTIS. In this novel, he wrote of an Invisible College along the lines of the Rosicrucian teachings. In fact, much of his novel had a distinct Rosicrucian bent. This novel actually was the impetus for the founding of the Royal Society by the Order of the Rosy Cross during the reign of Charles II[94].

There are many who believe that Bacon led what amounted to a double life. As alluded to earlier, many suspected that he was actually the author of the plays of William Shakespeare. Bacon was highly placed in the Elizabethan Court and this court, as Bacon often remarked was one where poetry and the theatre were scorned. So it was felt that he would naturally hide his authorship behind the name of another.

Others even feel that Bacon was the real author of the works of other contemporary writers such as Edmund Spenser, Christopher Marlowe, and Robert Burton to name but a few. It is strange that none of the original manuscripts of the above named writers have ever been found. In fact, in the case of Shakespeare, none of his hand written originals has been found. For such a prolific writer, this would seem to be impossible.

---

[94] Ibid

Bacon himself, often alluded to the fact that he would be known for who he really was long after his death. Could it be that this early genius gave us some of our most remembered plays? Could those original manuscripts still be in existence today? This is a very real possibility.

In 1911, following clues that he said he found in some of Bacon's writings, Dr. Orville Ward Owen, an American Baconian from Detroit, headed an expedition to the mouth of the Wye River near Gloucester, England. He believed that he had discovered an underground hiding place, beneath the riverbed, prepared by Bacon to hold secrets not meant for release to the Elizabethan World. What he found, after much searching was a room sized vault made of stone and cement. Unfortunately, it was empty.

However, several thousand miles away was a similar hiding place that some now credit to Bacon as another cache of his works. The mysterious treasure of Oak Island. In 1920, much evidence was found that could well link the research of Francis Bacon in the preservation of books and the Oak Island Treasure. Bacon wrote of using Mercury to preserve books over long periods of time and many Elizabethan Era containers that had contained Mercury were found in a trash dump on the Island. Could one of the greatest minds of history, and a probable member of several secret societies have created that engineering marvel of Oak Island? Only when someone can manage to defeat the brilliance of the engineers who built the "Money Pit" will we know for sure[95]. How can we be sure of Bacon's secret society membership? The title pages of many of Bacon's works featured Masonic symbols and other symbols of various secret societies. Could this be a definite clue to his affiliations? It was through these works that Bacon became one of the most influential writers of his day, an influential individual who was intent on spreading his occult philosophy.

ROYAL CHARTER

In 1606, King James I set up the Virginia Company which was granted the power to begin settlements in the province of Virginia. In 1607, Jamestown was founded as the first settlement in Virginia. It is interesting to note who the early members of the Virginia Company actually were. These were aristocrats who supported the Church of England and the Royalist cause. Among this number were:

- Lord Southampton
- Earl of Pembroke

---

[95] O'Connor, D'Arcy, THE BIG DIG, Ballantine Books, New York. 1978, 1988

- Earl of Montgomery
- Earl of Salisbury
- Earl of Northampton
- Sir Francis Bacon (1609) also Chancellor

This creating of the colonies was actually the first step towards the American Revolution. For even though Bacon allegedly owed his loyalties to King James, he actually helped found the colonies in order that they would one day break from the motherland and form a democratic society. A democratic society that Bacon felt would be a power base from which certain hidden forces could arise to change the world to conform to his ideas of world order.

This use of political office to carry out personal plans is a classic example of a government official placing his secret society goals above his loyalty to his government. In a speech to parliament, Bacon referred to the founding of the colonies as the establishment of Solomon's House in America. A clear reference to Masonic symbolism[96], as Solomon's House is a reference to the Temple of Solomon.

It is interesting to note that several members of Bacon's family actually settled in the new world. They may have been the literal trail blazers for the Puritan Sect who came in

---

[96] Howard, Michael, THE OCCULT CONSPIRACY, Destiny Books. Rochester, Vermont. 1989.

1620. Interestingly enough, there is evidence that the first Masonic Lodges in this Country were formed in 1620. From this date forward, Masonic influence was strong in the colonies. This influence would become so strong that only six (6) of the fifty-six (56) signers of the Declaration of Independence were not Masons[97].

COLONIAL ECONOMIC FREEDOM

In the beginning, the Colonies had economic freedom. The various Colonies issued their own script as well as allowed the money of various nations that traded with the Colonies to be used as mediums of exchange. This meant that the Colonial economy was not only sound, but also self-contained and growing. The English merchants also took the Colonial mediums of exchange as payment for goods shipped to Colonial ports.

This was a sound system, but it meant that the Colonies were able to stand on their own two feet financially. This was not viewed as a good thing by certain influential powers in England. It was decided by these influential powers that steps were to be taken to put a stop to this. However, these steps had to be taken very circumspectly. The first step was to get control of the

---

[97] Ibid

English Monarchy and the British money supply.

THE FIRST MOVE TOWARD REVOLUTION

Most of the colonists were loyal to England and their King. Had the English government governed, instead of allowing others to dictate to it, the United States would probably be a British satellite today. However, in 1694, William III was in desperate need of cash. A group of wealthy Englishmen, under the leadership of William Paterson formed the "Company of the Bank of England" and offered to loan King William one million, two hundred thousand pounds (about six million dollars) at eight per cent interest on condition that the Bank of England be empowered to issue notes to the full extent of its capital[98].

Paterson later wrote that *"If the proprietors of the Bank can circulate their own fundation of twelve hundred thousand (1,200,000) pounds without having more than two or three hundred thousand pounds lying dead at one time with another, this Bank will be in effect as nine hundred thousand pounds or a million in fresh money brought into the nation."*

In other words, what the King gave the Bank of

---

[98] Griffin, Des, FOURTH REICH OF THE RICH, Emissary Publications. 1984.

England was the power to create money from nothing. In return for the loan of twelve hundred thousand pounds, the Bank got the right to take 1,200,000 pounds and turn it into 2,400,000 pounds. One half in gold and one half in script. And collect interest in that loaned to the King. Not a bad deal. The result of this action by the King was to give control of the English economy to a private group.

One area that should be examined is who were William Paterson and his "group of wealthy Englishmen"? To whom did King William turn over control of the English money supply? It is to be supposed that King William had never heard the statement, *"It matters not who sits on the throne, but he who controls the money actually rules"*.

Research has shown that William Paterson was a Scot. Is it a mere coincidence that the idea that he proposed to King William was the very same fractional reserve system that had been developed by the Knights Templar? Remember that members of the Knight Templar sought refuge among the Scots and later fought for Scottish National Sovereignty. In fact, it was a Templar charge against the center of the English line that turned the tide for the Scottish forces in the last war between English and Scottish Royalty.

Is it possible that Paterson was a descendant of one

of the intermarriages between Templar and native Scot? The Templars were well versed in the Middle Eastern traditions of conquer your enemies by appearing to join them. An Englishman, or any other race for that matter, can sit on the throne, but if you control the purse strings, then you control the kingdom.

Where would the Scots have gotten the funds to form the Company of the Bank of England, when the Country itself was so impoverished? Remember that the entire Templar treasury disappeared along with the Templar fleet and many of the high officials of the Order. Did the Templar treasury reappear in the form of the Bank of England?

THE MONEY POWERS THAT BE

This situation proved that money could be created. This method of creating money used by the Bank of England was actually the fore runner of our own "fractional reserve system" instituted by the Federal Reserve System[99]. The major problem seen by critics was that this power to create money was in private hands, not those of government.

As with most bankers, the powers behind the Bank of England were concerned, not with the public good, but

---

[99] Greider, William, SECRETS OF THE TEMPLE, Touchstone Books. New York. 1987.

with profit. The philosophy of the Bank of England seemed to be "If profits were good during good times, then they should be even better during bad times." And as with all bankers, the Bank of England soon discovered that it had the power to create the "bad times".

Once they had control of the economy, this "Group of Wealthy Englishmen" soon had control of the King. It was through this control of the King, that the "powers behind the scenes" planned to regain financial control of the Colonies.

Thus in 1720, the English Government put out instructions to all Royal Governors to allow no more printing of colonial currency without a suspending clause. As a result, by 1738 the colonial currency had become so devalued as against English money that English merchants really didn't want to take it in exchange. At the same time the mother country was having financial troubles, the colonies were undergoing unparalled prosperity[100].

The main reason that the Bank of England wanted to stop the colonists from using their own money was that by not using English currency, the colonists didn't have to pay interest to the European Bankers for the privilege of using it.

---

[100] Griffin, Des, FOURTH REICH OF THE RICH, Emissary Publications. 1984.

In 1751, the British Board of Trade submitted a bill to Parliament to ban Colonial Currency in New England. This resulted in the Colonists being forced to borrow from the European Bankers. In 1764, this ban was extended to the rest of the Colonies[101].

Our history books talk a great deal about unfair taxation as being at the base of the Revolutionary War. Actually, the real reason for the war was the revoking of the power to create money that the colonies originally had been granted. The true facts were that the money powers, the Bank of England and the powers behind them, had gained control over all of Britain and then tried to extend that power to this country.

THE PLAN

The plan of the Bank of England was clearly to try and drown the colonies in a mountain of debt. No less a figure than Benjamin Franklin stated that *"The Plan of our adversaries is to render the Assemblies in America useless. . .It is in our interests to prevent this."*

Exorbitant prices were placed on goods shipped to the colonies. The Bankers had forced an over production situation in England which made the actual cost of items

---

[101] Ibid

shipped to the colonies extremely cheap. Then the colonists were forced to pay dearly for these same items once they were shipped. The results were massive profits for those on the "inside". At the same time, the law required the colonists to pay for the products in "hard money", (i.e. specie or gold and silver coins) This had the additional results of draining the colonies of hard money gained through trade with other countries.

To further enslave the colonists, Parliament then passed a law forbidding trade by the colonies with other countries. All goods must be purchased from England. This forced the colonies to borrow from the Bankers and again this added to their profits.

In order to try and survive, the Colonies decided to band together. In 1774, the first Continental Congress was convened in order to try and come to a solution. In October, 1774, the Declaration of Resolution was issued. A boycott was organized of British goods. England then forbade trading between England and the colonies which effectively isolated the Colonies.

In spite of the fact that the Crown was slowly strangling the colonies, there had been no talk of breaking away from the mother country. The colonists were still loyal to their King. The impetus for the revolution actually came from England. On August 23, 1775, King George III, on advice from his aides and in answer to demands from the Bankers, issued a Proclamation of Rebellion. It was actually King George III who started the American Revolution. Each side continued to escalate the matter until July 4, 1776, when the Declaration of Independence was signed.

This seemed to be a revolution that no one intended. As far as the colonists were concerned, they were Englishmen. It was the manipulations and exploitations of the Bankers that forced the split.

THE UNSEEN HAND

The Major question that I have is, was the Revolution planned by the secret societies? There is much evidence that the International Bankers were organized at a very early stage as a force to be reckoned with. According to most writers and researchers on this topic, the foremost of the International Banking powers was the Rothschild Family. In a later chapter, we shall look at this remarkable family more closely, but for now suffice it to say that it was the International Bankers that actually manipulated the American Colonies into splitting from the Motherland. Therefore, it is logical to ask if this was all part of some plan.

A careful study of the American Revolution reveals that the influence of Freemasonry was pervasive. For example, St. Andrew's lodge in Boston was involved in the so-called Boston Tea Party and John Hancock, first Continental Congress President was a member.

Even the colonial rallying cry of liberty, equality, brotherhood, tolerance and the talk about the rights of man were actually directly out of Masonic teachings. It was also the cry echoed by the French Revolutionists. Even the philosophy of the day as it filtered its way to the common private of the line in both the American and British Armies was Masonic in content. Surprisingly enough, every major Army unit on both sides had a Masonic Lodge incorporated into it. I was also surprised to find that this situation is still true today. If ever a country was dominated with Masonic teachings, it was the fledgling United States[102].

Even though history makes it look as if it was the outstanding accomplishments of George Washington that made him the unanimous choice for Commanding General of the Continental Army, this is not true. He had several opponents who competed with him for the top position. It was actually Masonic influence that resulted in George

---

[102] Baigent, Michael and Richard Leigh, THE TEMPLE AND THE LODGE, Arcade Publishing. New York. 1989.

Washington being appointed Commander of the Continental Army and later President of the United States.

According to contemporary writers, most of Washington's military staff were Masons and letters of introduction to Washington from prominent Masons could result in a commission as an officer much quicker than Congressional Appointment. It was also Masonic influence and assistance that resulted in professional soldiers arriving to help train the new Army such as Pulaski and Lafayette. It could almost be said that without the Masonic brotherhood, there would be no United States.

Interestingly enough, the British commanders were also Masonic members. This brotherhood among both armies resulted in some almost comic and many unbelievable happenings as Brother Mason appealed to Brother Mason in the heat of battle. Many "miraculous" happenings are the result of Masonic assistance. Even the British Army's closest allies, the Mohawks were not immune to Masonic appeals. The Chief of the Mohawks, Joseph Bryant, was himself a Mason.

So up to this point, we have seen the influence of several different Secret Societies in the creation of this great country and in the events that led up to the Revolution. As we will examine in greater detail in a future book, each of these secret societies was at one time a part of an even older order. But for now you must be content with the knowledge that this is true. Many could and have argued that the events described above just happened, that there was and is no conspiracy. Naturally in this book, I do not have sufficient space to examine this time period in detail, however, in the next chapter, the unseen hand and the underground conspiracy become much more apparent.

THE LARGER PICTURE

However, at the same time that the British and European Bankers were trying to strangle the Colonies, there were many other things happening in the world. Historically, the late 1700's and early 1800's were a time of great activity by many secret societies.

The following are but a few happenings from this time period[103]:

- **1701-** War of Spanish Succession begins. Iroquois Confederacy makes treaties with both the English and the French.
- **1702-** Queen Anne's War begins in America.
- **1706-** Benjamin Franklin Born.

---

[103] Wilgus, Neal, THE ILLUMINOIDS, Sun Books, New Mexico, 1978.

- **1707-** Buffon and Saint-Germain born.
- **1708-** William Pitt Born.
- **1710-** St. Germaine (famous alchemist) allegedly born.
- **1712-** Frederick II and Rousseau born.
- **1713-** Queen Anne's War ends.
- **1714-** War of Spanish Succession ends.
- **1717-** Founding of Modern Freemasonry with the Grand Lodge of London.
- **1721-** Masonry introduced to France.
- **1723-** Anderson's Constitutions of the Freemasons published. Also publication of Ebrietatis Enconium and other anti-masonic books published.
- **1724-** Publication of anti-Masonic "Grand Mysteries of the Freemasons Discovered".
- **1727-** Benjamin Franklin founds "Leather Apron Society", a secret society similar to Masons.
- **1728-** Masonry introduced to Spain.
- **1729-** Catherine II born.
- **1730-** Masonry introduced to America and India.
- **1731-** Franklin initiated into Masonry. The Leather Apron Society became the Junto Club and later became the American Philosophical Society.
- **1732-** George Washington born.

- **1733-** War of Polish Succession began.
- **1734-** Franklin elected Grand Master of Pennsylvania. Masonry introduced to the Netherlands.
- **1735-** Masonry introduced into Portugal, Russia and Italy.
- **1736-** Masonry introduced into Switzerland.
- **1737-** Thomas Paine born. Masonry introduced into Germany.
- **1738-** George III born. Masonry introduced into Turkey. Anti-Masonic Papal Edict issued. Apology for the Free and Accepted Masons published.
- **1739-** Masonry introduced into Poland.
- **1740-** Maria Teresa become Queen of Austria, Bohemia, and Hungary; Frederick II becomes King of Prussia, invades Austria; War of Austrian succession begins.
- **1743-** Cagliostro, Thomas Jefferson, Marat and Meyer Rothschild born. Masonry introduced to Australia and Denmark.
- **1744-** King George's War begins in America.
- **1748-** Adam Weishaupt born. King George's War ends, War of Austrian Succession ends.
- **1752-** George Washington initiated into Masonry.

- **1754-** Louis XVI born. French and Indian War begins. Adam Weishaupt begins training with Jesuits. Elect Cohens, forerunner of Illumines or Martinists founded by Martines de Pasqually of Paris.
- **1756-** Seven Years War begins.
- **1757-** Appearance of Skoptsi or Castrator Sect in Russia.
- **1760-** George III become King of England.
- **1761-** Chinese Emperor issues edict against Secret Societies.
- **1762-** Illumines of France founded. Catherine II overthrows Peter III in Russia.
- **1763-** Seven Years War ends. French and Indian War ends with French losing all American colonies.
- **1765-** British Stamp Act imposed to help pay for French and Indian War debt. Sons of Liberty clubs formed to resist tax.
- **1766-** Stamp Act repealed. Illuminati of Avignon founded by Pernety.
- **1767-** Townshend Revenue Act, another British Tax on Colonies. Elect Cohens introduced to Lyons.
- **1768-** Virginia legislature dissolved by Royal Governor for its opposition to Townshend Act.

Weishaupt graduates from the University of Ingolstadt.

- **1769-** Napoleon born.
- **1770-** Boston massacre: British troops fire into a crowd. Townshend Act repealed except for tea tax.
- **1771-** Amalgamation of all French Masonic Lodges into the Amis Reunis. Russian Government discovers existence if the Skoptsi.
- **1772-** Grand Orient of France founded. First Colonial Committee of Correspondence founded in Boston by Samuel Adams. California, New Mexico and Texas become Interior Provinces of Spanish Colonies. Cossack Rebellion in Russia. Tay Son Brothers start rebellion against Nguyen Family in Vietnam.
- **1773-** Amschel Rothschild born. British Tea Tax on Colonies; Boston Tea Party. Weishaupt marries. Meyer Rothschild and others meet to plan a world revolution. Suppression of the Jesuits. Decline of the Ancient and Noble Order of the Bucks, early version of the Odd Fellows. Pugachov uprising in Russia begins.
- **1774-** William Morgan and Solomon Rothschild born. Britain's "Intolerable Acts" designed to punish

the colonies. First Continental Congress; Washington begins training troops. Louis XV dies, Louis XVI becomes King of France.

- **1775-** Second Continental Congress authorizes naval warships, sets up secret committee to procure weapons, names Washington commander in chief of the American Army. George III proclaims America in open rebellion. Battles of Lexington, Bunker Hill, and Ticonderoga. Beginning of the "Guerse de Farines" in which the people instigated by the Prince of Conti and other Masons, invade Versailles begging for bread from Louis XVI.

- **1776-** Illuminati founded by Adam Weishaupt. American Declaration of Independence adopted by Continental Congress.

- **1777-** Nathan Rothschild born. Weishaupt joins Munich Lodge of Theodore of Good Council. Articles of Confederation adopted by Continental Congress.

- **1778-** France recognizes American Independence. Conway Cabal plots to replace Washington.

- **1780-** Weishaupt's wife dies. Cagliostro and Knigge Illuminated, Illuminati begins rapid growth.

- **1781-** Cornwallis surrendered at Yorktown. John

Hanson becomes first President of the United States in Congress Assembled.

- **1782**- British Cabinet agrees to recognize American Independence, agreement signed in Paris. Hanson commissions great deal and finishes term. Elias Boudinot elected second President of Congress Assembled.
- **1783**- Treaty signed between America and England; Washington disbands Army and resigns. Hanson dies. Thomas Mifflin elected third President of Congress Assembled.
- **1784**- Treaty with England ratified by Congress. Richard Henry Lee elected fourth President of congress Assembled.
- **1785**- Weishaupt flees to Gotha; New Edict Outlaws Illuminati; Lanz struck by lighting and Illuminati papers found.
- **1786**- Police raids uncover Illuminati papers in homes of Zwack and Bassus. Mirabeau illuminated by Mauvillon. Secret Congress held in Frankfurt where Louis XVI and Gustavus III of Sweden are condemned to die by Illuminati. Nathaniel Gorham elected fifth President of Congress Assembled.
- **1787**- German Union formed by Bahrdt as a

successor of the Illuminati. Washington elected president of the Continental Convention; new constitution adopted by the convention. Arthur St. Clair elected sixth President of Congress Assembled. Thomas Jefferson went to Paris to meet with a Brazilian rebel to discuss American aid to the revolution in Brazil.

- **1788**- Byron, Fresnel and Carl Rothschild born. American Constitution is ratified by the states. Cyrus Griffin is elected seventh President of Congress Assembled.

- **1789**- Washington elected President; first congress under the new Constitution. French Revolution begins, fall of the Bastille.

- **1790**- Rebellion and massacre throughout France. Franklin dies.

- **1791**- Louis XVI attempts to escape and is arrested. Thomas Paine writes Rights of Man in England. The anonymous work, Vie de Joseph Balsamo linking Illuminati and the French Revolution appears.

- **1792**- James Rothschild born. Washington re-elected. War between France and Austria. Paris mobs attack the Kings Palace; Swiss Guard is massacred, Monarchy overthrown. Assassination of

King Gustavus III of Sweden.

- **1793-1795-** French Republic. Hundreds of thousands die.
- **1795-** French Directory begins.

The last decades of the 18th century were wars, rebellions, mobs death and destruction. The old order was almost forced to its knees. Coincidence? Or perhaps the culmination of a phase of a long established and long running plan carried out by a secret order older than civilization.

As history has shown, this secret order is not infallible nor is it always victorious. It is simply patient, wealthy and willing to work and wait for ultimate victory. So let us now move ahead in our examination and look at some of the major players.

CHAPTER EIGHT

THE PLAYERS

This act (The Federal Reserve Act) establishes the most gigantic trust on earth... When the President signs this act the invisible government by the money powers, proven to exist by the Money Trust Investigation, will be legalized. Charles A. Lindbergh Sr.

In order to thoroughly study, and understand, what makes up the Eternal Conspiracy today, it is necessary to look at the major players. The names of individuals may change, but the same family groups and organizations tend to pop up from year to year.

In order to completely control a populace, there are certain areas that must be dominated:

1. Finance
2. Religion
3. Manufacturing

4. The Media
5. Politics

Part of what we are going to do in this and the volumes to follow is to study how the Eternal Conspiracy has been able to control society as a whole. They have been able to do this through various organizations designed to expedite control. One of the major groups involved in this Conspiracy, in fact this particular group was probably formed in order to further the Conspiracy, has been a uniquely European Institution called the Merchant Bankers that has allowed them to control world finance.

WHEN IS A BANK NOT A BANK?

A Merchant Bank is not a Bank as is understood by the majority of the American people. In the United States a Bank is a privately owned, governmentally regulated institution designed (allegedly) to serve its depositors. A Merchant Bank, on the other hand, is a privately owned institution that is not regulated by any agency and is usually used to manipulate investments on behalf of the owners and their clients.

The basis of the Rothschild Family power has been a chain of Merchant Banks. Through this chain, they have been able to form an unbelievable network of cooperating banks. This cooperation among Bankers has enabled the Rothschilds to amass what is probably the largest fortune in the known world.

As a result of this chain of cooperating banks and partial ownership (and usual total control) of various nations central banks, the Rothschilds have been able to dictate financial policy the world over. Naturally when you control the world's money supply, you also control manufacturing, national financial policy, and to a lesser extent, finance and the media.

POLITICAL PLAYERS

There are only a few internationally known political figures. I am not talking about elected figures, but I am talking about the few international politicians that have changed the world's political spectrum. It is most interesting to discover that each of these International, all powerful figures owe their position in one shape form or fashion to the Rothschild Family.

But, less I steal my own thunder, instead of listening to me talk about these people, in generalities, read on and see the details of the backgrounds and histories of some of the world's most private and powerful forces.

FINANCIAL RULERS

It would have been impossible for the Conspiracy to have made the inroads that it has into society without an almost virtual control over the finances of the effected countries. The Conspiracy of which I write buys who and what it wants. This conspiracy offers more to its members than just the hope of future power. It also offers immediate rewards that can be beyond your wildest imagination.

As a prime example, a second rate unknown politician, from an obscure town in Georgia can become President of the United States. A B grade actor who hasn't made a major movie in some years can become Governor of one of our most powerful States and then President of the United States if he has the right backing.

If you are unprincipled enough to desire to be part of the Conspiracy, then the conspiracy can and in most cases, does, make many of your dreams come true. But there is no free lunch; there is a price for this bounty. Just remember, you will always be owned by the conspiracy, just like someone who deals with the Mafia.

To add to the confusion, there is even some question as to who or what makes up the conspiracy. Many writers seem to feel that the International Bankers are the top level of the Conspiracy and everyone else works for them. This is most definitely not true.

The Conspiracy, by whatever name you wish to call it, has been in existence for many, many centuries. During this period of time, the Conspiracy bought, and operated through, Kings, Princes and Popes. The International Bankers have only been an effective tool since the late 1600's. However, it is true that since that time, the International Bankers have been the major force that has brought most of the world under the control of the Conspiracy.

The Elite Insiders of the Conspiracy are individuals who are above suspicion. These are not the side walk agitators of 1917 Russia, nor the Karl Marx's' freezing in a garret while re-writing what became known as the Communist Manifesto. No, these Insiders are the super-rich, but totally anonymous manipulators of countries around the world. The Elite do not soil their hands with killing and oppression, but instead, they open their checkbooks and pay to have their enemies killed. But, in spite of their "clean hands" their guilt is certain, nonetheless.

In their drive for world domination, the Elite Insiders have used many tools. Some tools are useful for only a short time, such as a Richard Nixon, or a Jimmy Carter while other tools are useful for much longer, such as an Edmond

Rothschild. But sooner or later, each tool has outlived its' usefulness and is discarded. Only the Elite, themselves, go on indefinitely.

THE ELITE

There are many in the world who point to the Jewish Race as being the cause and center of the Eternal Conspiracy. Allegedly this is the reason for the continual oppression that the Jewish people have undergone for centuries. Literally hundreds of books and articles have been written making the Jewish Race, as a whole, appear to be involved in the conspiracy. However, as I pointed out earlier, this is simply not true. The Jewish people, as a whole, are no more responsible for the beginnings of the Eternal Conspiracy that is Santa Claus.

Granted that it is true that many members of the Elite of the Eternal Conspiracy are of the Jewish Race, but this is about as relevant as saying that because most Republicans are Caucasian that the Republican Party is a Caucasian Party. These are simply facts of life. However, the fact that so many Jews are members has been used as a screen to point those who would look away from the truth.

THE POWER CENTER

One cannot discuss the power of the Elite Insiders without the discussion coming around to the City of London. Not the London, England that we are familiar with, but the City, a one mile square enclave within the actual confines of the modern City of London. This one square mile of earth is where the financial power of this planet is consolidated. Within the confines of the City of London, even the Queen of England must bend knee to the Mayor of the City. It is from this power center that the Elite Insiders control much of their empire.

For so small an area, the City wields a totally unbelievable amount of political and financial power. Many are certain that this is the seat of the secret world super government. It is also believed that from this seat of power, all political and financial actions are monitored by this colossal organization[104].

In 1874, Walter Bagehot, one of the best known Victorian Bankers, called the City of London "by far the greatest combination of economical power and economical delicacy that the world has ever seen." On the surface, the City (always capitalized) has lost some of its power, but it

---

[104] Knuth, E.C., THE EMPIRE OF THE CITY, The Noontide Press, P.O. Box 1248, Torrance, CA 90505. 1983.

still controls much of the financial world[105]. There is more money made and lost in the City than Wall Street has ever dreamed of. It provides the so called "invisible earnings", estimated to be in excess of two hundred million pounds a year that helps Britain's balance of payments.

The City of London has a way of life that has gone unchanged for some five hundred years. The City has some very bizarre rules, but if you understand them and abide by them a fortune can be made. Some of these rules are hopelessly outdated, but if you try to change them, chaos would result.

For example, the Bank of England is still guarded every night by a detachment of the Brigade of Guards, who each day in full dress uniform, march there to the sound of drums. History records that this detachment of the Brigade of Guards has marched there each day since 1780, when a mob tried to storm the Bank. While there has not been any further trouble of that nature since 1780, but the Bank of England wants its Guards[106].

It is in the narrow twisting streets of the City of London where the operational arms of the conspiracy can be found usually operating out of a peculiar firm known as a

---
[105] Wechsberg, Joseph,. THE MERCHANT BANKERS, Little Brown and Co., Boston, Toronto.1966.
[106] Ibid

Merchant Bank. Not a true Bank in the terms that most of us think of in the United States, but a Bank in the European tradition. But make no mistake, these are very powerful institutions.

It was through the creation of the Merchant Banks and the various central banks of the many countries that the Conspiracy was able to utilize its' most potent weapons, an inflatable currency. This creation has been the means of enslaving us all.

Who, individually, actually started the original Conspiracy is a matter of conjecture. But whoever he, or she, was, they planned well. This Conspiracy has been so effective and so secret that even today, many do not believe it exists, even though it has its' foot on the throat of us all. One master stroke was gaining control of the economy of the various major countries. For as we have observed before, if you control the money, especially an inflatable currency, you in the end, control the controllers. Therefore, one important tool that would be required for total domination would be the creation of or control of one of the major banking house. Just such a creation was the House of Rothschild.

THE ROTHSCHILD FAMILY

Naturally, no book on International Bankers, nor the Conspiracy for that matter, can be complete without discussing the most effective tool the Conspiracy has forged in centuries, the Rothschild Family. No Family has profited more from their involvement with the Conspiracy nor has any one family done more for the Conspiracy than this International Banking Family. From a minor cog in the infant wheel of international finance, in a few short years, the Rothschild family was a major force in the western financial world.

The Rothschild Family has been useful in several ways, as follows:

1.) Gave conspiracy researchers a visible target, i.e. International Bankers. Many have mistaken the tool for the user. In other words, many have come to believe that the International Bankers were the Conspiracy. This has been useful in taking the spotlight off of the real powers. As I observed before, the International bankers have done much to move the world toward a one world government, but their moves were all part of a grand design created by another.

2.) Since the Rothschilds are Jewish, (Meyer Amschel

was a Hassidic Jew, among the most fanatical. He believed that God has promised the Jews the rulership of the earth) many have come to believe that the Conspiracy is a totally Jewish Plot. It is true that many of the visible power brokers are Jewish, but I think that this is more coincidence than design. For some reason, members of the Jewish race do tend to gravitate towards centers of financial power, have no qualms about manipulating matters to their advantage and are probably among the more ruthless of Bankers, but to describe the creation of such a vast century spanning Conspiracy as being totally Jewish in nature is to overlook many of the facts.

The religious affiliations of the Elite Insiders cover the gamut from Jewish to Catholic and everything in between. But it is useful as a distraction to have the world believe that the Conspiracy is purely a Jewish creation.

3.) Gave the Elite Insiders a willing, useful tool to almost virtually control the finances of the Western World.

However, make no mistake about it, the Rothschild Family, important as it is, is nothing more than hired help as far as the real Insiders are concerned. For without the help of the Elite Insiders, the Rothschild Family would probably not have the International Power that it does today.

The first reference to the Rothschild Family that can be found is dated 1585 and mentions Isaak Elchanan at the Red Shield (the word Rothschild actually means red shield). From this date until the early 1700's, the family trade was principally retailing. But in the early years of the 18th century, the family became money changers. Additionally, unlike many Jewish Families living in Frankfort-On-The-Main, they were not poor, but reasonably well off[107].

In 1755, when Meyer Amschel (the name Rothschild was actually adopted by Meyer Amschel at a later date) was twelve, his father and mother died, leaving him an inheritance. So at an early age, he was thrown on his own to sink or swim.

Due to the chaotic conditions prevailing in Germany during these years, there were many opportunities available for someone who was smart and had a little money. Since Meyer Amschel had been employed by his father since age ten in money changing, he had a very good idea of the usefulness of money and also was able to spot the occasional

---

[107] Count Egon Caesar Corti, THE RISE OF THE HOUSE OF ROTHSCHILD, Western Islands, L.A. CA.1972.

rare and valuable coin that came into his hands. Additionally, since Germany was so divided into small countries, before anyone would depart on a trip of any length, they had to go to the money changer to have their coins changed into the currency of the country for which they were bound.

Meyer Amschel first went to work for the firm of Oppenheim at Hanover. During this time he made the acquaintance of General von Estorff, a coin collector, who paid the young man to find rare coins for the General. Since the General was connected with the ruling house of Hesse, Meyer Amschel saw a chance to use this new connection.

Later, Meyer Amschel's contacts with the General and his knowledge of Coin collecting resulted in Meyer being brought into contact with Prince William of Hesse, son of Frederick II of Hesse, grandson of King George III of England and son-in-law of King Frederick V of Denmark who was also married to a daughter of King George III of England.

In 1769, Meyer Amschel used his contacts with the Prince to petition for a title, a title in those days being very useful. The petition was granted and so on September 21, 1769, to the name Rothschild was attached the title, "Crown Agent to the Principality of Hesse-Hanau." The title stood him in good stead, opening several doors that would have been closed otherwise.

Prince William, Meyer Amschel's benefactor had married before Meyer did, but found that he had little liking for his bride. Meyer, on the other hand took a bride he deeply cared for and founded a family. Prince William founded several lines, all illegitimate. The Haynau, Heimrod, and Hessenstein lines are all descended from Prince William.

Prince William was known for his very broad religious views, associated much with Masons and practiced complete religious tolerance. However, he was a very smart business man. Following in the footsteps of his father, Prince William sold his own Regiment to England in 1776. As a result of his sharp business dealings, the Crown Prince cleared a profit of 3,500,000 marks from his "selling" of soldiers.

These funds were managed for the Prince by the Amsterdam financial house, Van der Notten. Often England would pay in Bills of Exchange, which had to be discounted. This task was handled for the Prince by another Jewish agent, Veidel David[108]. At this time, Meyer Amschel Rothschild was a very small fish indeed.

In 1785, the Prince's father Frederick II died, leaving the

---

[108] Ibid

Prince a fortune of an unheard of amount and the throne of Hesse-Cassel. The Prince continued to conduct international business, but used tried and true agents, not Rothschild. It was not until 1790, that Rothschild's father-in-law brought him together with a Crown Treasury official named Buderus.

Buderus had become the Prince's favored treasury official when he found a way to increase the Prince's income from one of the Prince's dairies. As a sign of the Prince's favor, Buderus was entrusted with the accounts of the Prince's private purse. It was Buderus who was responsible for the creation of the Salt Tax, which greatly increased the Prince's revenues. Naturally, after the introduction by his father-in-law, Rothschild sought out Buderus and made a great friend of him. It was this friend, Buderus, who finally convinced the Prince to entrust Rothschild with the handling of some of his bigger accounts.

It was the French Revolution that actually began the real rise to prominence of the Rothschild Family. As a result of the confusion caused by the execution of the King of France, and Napoleon's later rise to power, the political climate in Europe drastically changed. Additionally, it was the conquering of Holland by the French in 1795 that caused the greatest of good fortune for the Bankers of Frankfort. The Amsterdam Bourse, which had handled much of the

European financial transactions up until that time, almost totally collapsed as a result of the invasion by the French. This brought the bulk of the business to Frankfort and the Bankers of this city. Foremost among them to receive business was Meyer Amschel Rothschild[109].

Rothschild had raised a large family, which now stood him in good stead. Instead of being forced to hire strangers into his business, Rothschild put his children, and their spouses, to work. As a result, the inter-workings of the Rothschild bank stayed confidential.

Prince William, after withdrawing from the war against the French, became a banker to most of the European World. In the negotiating of these loans, Jewish middlemen were normally used. Soon the Rothschilds were acting as the liaisons between many of the rulers of the day. Their influence was spreading, as was their fortunes. Between 1795 and 1800, Rothschild's assessed wealth went from 2,000 gulden to over a million gulden. Quite an increase for humble Jewish merchants.

In 1798, Meyer Amschel Rothschild's youngest son, Nathan, decided to move to London and open a branch of the family Bank. He took with him approximately twenty thousand pounds (or a quarter of a million gulden) as

---

[109] Ibid

funding for this first branch of the House of Rothschild. During the Napoleonic Period of France, the Paris office of the House of Rothschild was opened. The financial empire of the Rothschild Family was growing.

HOW TO PRESERVE THE FAMILY FORTUNE

When Meyer Amschel Rothschild died, he left a most unusual Will, which with the exception of a few key clauses has remained secret to this day. His Last Will and Testament was very specific in its instructions to his heirs. Penalties for failure to follow these instructions were severe. A few of the rules were as follows:

1. The eldest brother shall be the head and manager of the Rothschild wealth in its entirety. The rule of seniority does not exclude the rule of ability, but the latter can be applied only after a vote from the whole family.

2. Marriage shall be made within the family, among cousins, so that the wealth may not be divided or lost to outsiders.

3. The wealth shall remain undivided.

4. Meyer's will shall not be shown to anyone outside the family.

5. The Orthodox Jewish faith shall be kept by each and every member of the family.

6. All public inventories should be avoided and no inheritance suits should be filed among family members. Anyone who does not follow this rule shall be deprived of his inheritance.

7. The entire wealth, which is to remain undivided, shall be owned jointly by the family and managed only by the men. The women members of the family, as well as the husbands of the Rothschild's sisters do not have the right to participate in the firm's management.

By this Last Will and Testament, Meyer Amschel Rothschild intended to and did create a financial dynasty that now holds the world by the throat.

THE PROBLEMS WITH KINGS

As Meyer Amschel Rothschild had discovered, there

were fortunes to be made financing Kings. However, the lenders do face certain problems, such as what kind of collateral does a country give for a loan? What if the King has the Banker killed rather than pay off the loan?

According to economics Professor Stuart Crane, there are two means used to collateralize loans to governments. Just as a business gives up some control over its policies in return for loans, so governments have given up some political control in return for the billions upon billions of dollars that International Bankers have loaned over the years. Probably the most influential individuals in international politics are the International Bankers[110].

However, the ultimate advantage that an International Banker has is that if a country gets out of line, then the Banker can finance the enemies of that uncooperative country. This was a game that the Rothschild Family learned well how to play. Meyer Amschel Rothschild eventually had five sons and positioned them well. One ran the Frankfort Bank and the other four ran Banks in London, Paris, Vienna and Naples[111].

According to several authorities in the field of

---

[110] Allen, Gary and Larry Abraham., NONE DARE CALL IT CONSPIRACY, Double A Publications, Suite 403, 18000 Highway South, Seattle, Washington 98188..
[111] Ibid

economics, at the end of each war of the nineteenth century, there was a new structuring of the "balance of power" around the House of Rothschild in England, France and Austria. Each power block was used as a threat to keep the others in line and ensure that loans were repaid. Many of these wars of the nineteenth century were actually manipulated in order to "punish" countries or rulers who did not toe the Rothschild political line.

While the members of Rothschild Family were not the originators of this procedure of using the threat of war as a collection method, they did refine it to an art form. Over the centuries since the Rothschilds have become a power in the Conspiracy, millions have died so that the Rothschilds could be sure of making a profit.

CARL JOACHIM HAMBRO

Of course, the Rothschild Family was not the only family that the conspiracy worked with or through. Though the conspiracy does not want any competition, it will not, knowingly, create a monopoly for one of its' hired minions. After all, the conspiracy doesn't want any internal power struggles.

Of almost equal statute to the Rothschild Family is the Hambros Family. In fact, the Hambros Bank Ltd. is the world's largest Merchant Bank[112]. Naturally, the site of this major bank is in the famous City of London.

Hambros Bank Ltd. prides itself on being consciously unorthodox. It will cater for anything that involves money. The risks are unimportant, in fact, some of their greatest profits have been made from reverses to the British Empire. So how did this Bank get this attitude; indirectly from the United States.

Carl Joachim Hambros came to the United States in 1830, intending to work as a commercial apprentice. While here, he learned a new method of milling flour by the use of steam. This knowledge he promptly turned into money in Sweden. This began a tradition of investment in the U.S. market.

Like the Rothschilds, the Hambros made much of their fortune out of war and misery. It would seem that while the Rothschild's were at the center of the European dealing, the Hambros dealt with those that were not deemed important enough for the Rothschilds to support. It was as a result of funding the war that his native Denmark was having that Carl Hambros became Danish Baron Carl Hambros. In spite of this, Hambros Bank, Ltd. was still in the shadow of

---

[112] Wechsberg, Joseph,. THE MERCHANT BANKERS, Little Brown and Co., Boston, Toronto.1966.

Rothschilds. However, the Hambros were powerful enough to be called the "King Makers[113]".

It was with the help of Carl Joachim Hambros that Italy was unified and the Italian Royal Family was placed on its throne under King Victor Emmanuel. Without the financial support of the House of Hambros, the unification would have been impossible.

The revolutionaries in Italy were all working to forge a new country out of the several smaller warring states on the peninsula. However, as a simple fact of life, without funds, no new country can be born. The faction trying to unite the country sent representatives to England to ask for the help of the Rothschild Family. They were refused. Then they turned to Carl Hambros.

With the help of the Hambros Bank, Ltd. a bond issue was floated and funds were raised to allow the fight to be carried on to its conclusion. So it was that King Victor Emmanuel was eternally indebted to Carl Hambros.

Two years later, Carl Hambros again "stage managed" the placing of a second ruler on a throne. This time, the Country in question was Greece. In 1862, a revolution had deposed King Otto, son of King Ludwig of Bavaria.

---

[113] Ibid

The Greek people wanted Prince Alfred, second son of Queen Victoria as their new King. However, under an agreement, Great Britain, France and Russia had agreed that no member of their Royal Families would sit on the Greek Throne. Therefore, it was forbidden that Prince Alfred could possibly become King Alfred. Into the breach stepped Carl Hambros.

A Dane by birth, Carl Hambros used his influence and connections to suggest that the Greek emissaries look at Prince Wilhelm of Denmark. It just so happened that Prince Wilhelm "happened" to be visiting London at the same time the Emissaries were there. It was also strictly coincidence that Prince Wilhelm and Baron Hambros happened to attend the same church service that the Emissaries did and that they were able to get a good look at him. From this coincidence, Prince Wilhelm was offered the throne of Greece[114].

Though the evidence that Carl Hambros was involved in the conspiracy is circumstantial at best, it is a fact that Carl's oldest son, Everard, who became the sole owner of Hambros Bank, Ltd. after Carl's death in 1877, was a close friend of John Pierpont Morgan, a major Conspiracy member in the United States[115].

---

[114] Ibid
[115] Ibid

THE BARINGS.

Much less known that the Rothschilds, but probably as powerful is Baring Brothers & Co. Limited. At Two hundred and Two years old, it is the City of London's oldest Merchant Bank. The English Barings were founded in 1717 by a German, Johann Baring, who moved to Exeter in that year. Johann (later changed to John) Baring died in 1748 leaving four sons. It is these sons who developed the name Baring into a synonym for wealth and power.

Historically, the merchant bankers of London are the true descendants of the merchant traders of Venice. The wealth and power developed by these trading families was maintained by intermarriages between the merchant families and other wealthy families. In this way, truly unbelievable fortunes were created and maintained.

The Barings were the greatest international Bankers on the European scene long before the Rothschilds were even thought of as Bankers[116]. In fact, as recently as 1903, a German diplomat reported to the Foreign Office in Berlin that "anybody who wants to place a loan in London on a grand scale must apply to the Barings."

In other words, the Barings were some of the major powers on the European scene until recently, and are

---

[116] Ibid

probably still forces to be reckoned with in the financial world.

It has been said that the Bank of England is the "mother bank" of the international conspiracy. If this is true, then the Barings are still powerful forces, for no other Merchant Bank in London has sent as many directors to the Bank of England. These directors have been:

- Alexander Baring-1805
- Humphrey St. John Mildmay
- Thomas Baring
- Edward Charles Baring (First Baron Revelstoke)
- John Baring (Second Baron Revelstoke)
- Sir Edward Peacock
- George Rowland Stanley Baring (Third Earl of Cromer) appointed as Governor of the Bank of England in 1961.

The Baring family has five separate peerages, (Ashburn, Northbrook, Revelstoke, Cromer and Howick) and has been a major power both in the City and in Government for centuries. Using this power, the Barings have financed both sides of wars and have even been able to supply Britain's allies by sending shipments through the enemy's lines with impunity. The Barings even sent supplies to the American Colonies through the British blockade.

It was banking families such as the Barings, and they were, in fact, foremost among them all, that worked to make Britain a great mercantile power. It was, in turn, this mercantile power that allowed the founding of the British Empire.

Up until the American Civil War, the Barings were deeply involved in financial transactions in the United States. Almost all investment in the United States from England was handled by Barings as an intermediary.

It was the Barings that taught the United States Government the mechanism of influence and control that has been developed to an art in this Country.

In 1783, Francis Baring, the younger son of John Baring the founder of the English Barings, and partner in John and Francis Baring & Company in London (the firm that later became the Merchant Bank) opened a business in Philadelphia and became associated with the local business powers called the Philadelphia Group. Among the members of this group were Robert Morris, Thomas Willing, William Bingham and Robert Gilmore.

William Bingham was reportedly the richest man in America and it was he, who in 1793 offered Francis one and a quarter million acres in Maine at a cost of two shillings per acre. In 1795, Francis sent his son, Alexander to look the matter over and two years later, Alexander returned home with the land purchased, a new wife, Anne Bingham, William's daughter and a nine hundred thousand dollar dowry. It was also in 1795 that Barings became an international banker for the United States Government.

In 1798, the Barings assisted the United States in the undeclared war against France by purchasing armaments and shipping them to the United States. Then in 1802 when the Louisiana Purchase took place, it was the Barings that financed the transaction. The most interesting thing about this transaction was that at the time that Barings began to finance the deal, Britain was at war with France. Barings asked the British Government for permission to complete the transaction since it would give France much needed capital with which to conduct its war against Britain. However, in spite of the sheer lunacy of the request, which would aid Britain's enemy, Britain gave the deal the go ahead.

All in all, the Barings were the premier financiers until 1818 when they were the powers behind the sale of French Bonds. Shortly before this, France had been in grave need of raising capital in order to pay restitutions to the British arising out of the Napoleonic Wars. However, there was simply no money left in France. What France did have, however, was credit.

The French contacted Barings and worked out the deal for selling French Bonds. During two issues of bonds the deal made millions for all concerned. However, just prior to the third issue, the Rothschilds asked to have a piece of the pie. Barings was willing, but Hope & Co. of Amsterdam, the world's oldest merchant bank, and a partner in the bond deal, was not willing to let the upstart Rothschilds into the transaction.

In revenge, the Rothschilds used French money they were handling on other transaction for the European Powers to buy up the French Bonds forcing the price to rise. Naturally some of the leading statesmen of the day purchased the bonds. Then without notice, Rothschild's dumped their bonds on the market, forcing the price to drop like a rock. The future of the bonds was destroyed and hundreds of investors lost their investments. But the worst was that the Merchant Bank of Baring Brothers lost its place among the premier Merchant Banking Houses. They were eclipsed, from this time forth, by the House of Rothschild.

So began the dominance of the Rothschild Family that has lasted to this day. Has this dominance been beneficial to the world in general, or detrimental; read on and decide for yourself.

CHAPTER NINE

THE ROCKEFELLER DYNASTY

"Competition is a sin." John D. Rockefeller Sr.

There is much that is uncertain about the Rockefeller family. The line seemed to come from obscurity almost overnight. No one is even sure what their ethnic origins might be. According to one story, the Rockefellers are descended from French Protestants. Others believe that the family has a German origin, while still another theory, which seems to have much merit, is that the Rockefellers are actually Jewish in origin[117].

However, in checking some of the research found in THE ROCKFELLER FILE, referenced above, I went to Dr. Malcolm Stern's work entitled AMERICANS OF JEWISH DESCENT and found that indeed, the evidence made it appear that the Rockefeller Clan is probably of Jewish origin. Whatever may have been their origin, this family has come, in this last part of the twentieth century, to be one of

---

[117] Allen, Gary, THE ROCKEFELLER FILE, '76 Press, Seal Beach, CA.1976.

the dominate forces in world politics. Who are these financial rulers? When and how did they amass their wealth?

WILLIAM ROCKEFELLER

Grandfather of the current Rockefellers was William Rockefeller. Nicknamed "Doc", this Rockefeller was a traveling medicine man who sold bottles of petroleum, at $25.00 per pint, as a cure for warts, snake bite, cancer and numerous other ills. In other words, he was a traveling con man. It was this traveling con man that gave birth to the men who came to control America.

JOHN D. ROCKEFELLER SR.

John D. Rockefeller Sr. was probably the most intelligent of William's children. He also went on to become one of the most hated men in America due to his totally ruthless business moves. A deeply religious man, he proceeded to make a mockery of everything that he professed to believe in by destroying anyone and anything that stood in his way as he moved to the top.

It was in 1859 that John D. Rockefeller Sr. first became involved in the oil business. While still in his late teens, he had been a broker in Titusville, Pennsylvania, when his partners asked him to go look at the new oil business.

After his study, he decided that refining was the most profitable end of the business. It was at this time that he decided to start what became Standard Oil.

Standard Oil became the original basis of the Rockefeller fortune. To Rockefeller, the only efficient way to run a business was by having a monopoly. However, at the time he started Standard Oil, there were numerous competitors on the market. This was soon changed through the use of coercion, bribery, kickbacks and other underhanded schemes. Rumor also has it that when negotiations failed, John D. Rockefeller was not above a little violence when needed. Using these techniques, coupled with what appeared to be unlimited wealth (from an unknown source) Rockefeller built an empire that spanned the globe.

According to Ferdinand Lundberg in his book The Rich and the Super-Rich, "Rockefeller was of a deeply conspiratorial, scheming nature, always planning many years ahead." The characteristics described here are those that are mentioned when discussing the members of the conspiracy.

Additionally, this is the same advance planning always shown by the Conspiracy. Additionally, there are many rumors that the Rothschild Banks financed the original operation of Standard Oil. In other words, we have now come full circle and found the hand of the all-powerful Rothschild clan once again. Could the Rothschild Banks have been the source of Rockefeller's seemingly unlimited source of funds?

Most people think of oil when the name Rockefeller is mentioned, however, this commodity is now just a small cog in the Rockefeller machine. Let us look at the development of and some of the enterprises that the Rockefeller Empire encompasses.

- As an example of the wealth of Standard Oil (a.k.a. Standard Oil Trust, Standard Oil of New Jersey, Esso and Exxon) according to the February 18, 1974 of Time Magazine, this company declared annual profits of $2.4 Billion Dollars, the largest annual profits ever earned up to that time by any industrial company. Current figures for this company are seemingly hard to get for recent years.

- As of 1974, according to Fortune Magazine, if Exxon were shorn of is' foreign holdings it would still be the 9th largest industry in the United States.

- Individually and through family trusts, the

Rockefellers have effective working control over Mobil, Standard of Indiana, Standard of California and many other allegedly competing oil companies.

- The Rockefeller family controls First National City Bank (CitiCorp) and Chase Manhattan Bank (created by the merging of Rockefeller owned Chase Bank and the Kuhn, Loeb controlled Manhatten Bank).

As of 1971 Chase claimed $36 Billion in assets, but this only included assets directly owned by Chase, not the business conducted through affiliated banks.

Chase (as of 1974) had 28 foreign branches wholly owned by it and over 50,000 corresponding banks.

Chase is the only bank that has a full time envoy at the United Nations. The Chairman of chase has also met with heads of state and conducted international diplomacy on the same par as a head of state. A lot of power for a "simple" businessman.

- Chemical Bank of New York is yet another Rockefeller controlled institution. It is controlled by the Harkness Family, but Edward Harkness was one of John D. Rockefeller's closest associates.

- The Rockefeller Group of Banks is, as of 1974, heavily interlocked with the board of directors of Metropolitan Life, Equitable Life and New York Life. Control of these insurance companies gives the Rockefeller Group access to billions and billions of investment dollars through the assets of these three giant insurance companies.

- According to various sources (as of 1975), the following companies are owned (either through individual holdings of stock by the family or the family trusts), or controlled (through control of the major banks or "friendly boards) by the Rockefeller Group:

Exxon
Mobil Oil
Standard of CA
Standard of California
International Harvester
Inland Steel

Marathon Oil

Quaker Oats

Wheeling-Pittsburgh Steel

Freeport Sulphur

International Basic Economy Corporation

United Airlines

Northwest Airlines

Long Island Lighting

Atlantic Richfield Oil

National Airlines

IBM

Texaco

IT&T

Westinghouse

Boeing

International Paper

Minnesota Mining & Manufacturing

Sperry Rand

Xerox

National Cash Register

National Steel

American Home Products

Pfizer

Avon

Merck

Penn Central

TWA

Eastern

Delta

Braniff

Allied

Anaconda Copper

DuPont

Monsanto

Olin Mathison

Borden

National Distillers

Shell

Gulf

Union Oil

Dow

Celanese

Pittsburgh Plate Glass

Cities Service

Stauffer Chemical

Continental Oil

Union Carbide

American Cyanamid

American Motors
Bendix
Chrysler
C.I.T. Financial
S.S. Kresge
R.H. Macy

Consider that the above list is just those interests that are known about to the average reader of financial journals. What is not known about is the staggering amount of political power that the head of this financial dynasty can command. The fall of Khrushchev took place immediately after a Rockefeller "vacation" to Russia, at a time when tensions were at an all-time high. A coincidence?

CHAPTER TEN

THE GAMES BANKERS PLAY

"The tragedy of war is that it uses man's best to do man's worst." Ralph Waldo Emerson

In the last chapters, we have seen how the financial control of the world has become consolidated in the hands of a few International Powers. Each power linked to the other by both personal and business ties. So what has been the power of these particular International Bankers and how have they used this massive power? Would you believe that a few men have responsible for the changing of the social structure of their time? The very idea boggles the mind of the average man on the street. How can the activities of mere bankers change the social structure of the entire world? However, an astute reader of history can find the hidden hand of the International Bankers involved in several key situations in history.

There are many researchers who feel that the Eternal Conspiracy has taken control of various countries and used these countries for the carrying out of the wishes of the hidden powers. This is called the Conspiracy Theory of History by the liberal establishment and is ridiculed. However, again, an unbiased reading of history will all the astute reader to detect the manipulations of entire countries by forces that seem to be random in nature, but actually are highly sophisticated in their actions and effective in their programs.

The most obvious meddling with the social structure of the western world came during the late 1700's, when Agents of Meyer Amschel Rothschild instigated the French Revolution[118]. In order to get a clear picture of the situation as it was during the time of Meyer Amschel Rothschild, let's examine the events that led up to the French Revolution.

THE FRENCH REVOLUTION

King Louis XVI, in spite of the history books, was a good king. Upon assuming the throne, he began to institute many reforms designed to bring France out of the dark into the sun. He instituted many changes that both benefited his people and stripped the nobles of hereditary powers. The revolt that began in 1789 was started, not by the French

---

[118] Webster, Nesta H., THE FRENCH REVOLUTION, publisher unknown.

people, but by outside agitators financed by those who would maintain the status quo. The original leaders were, perhaps not surprisingly, all members of the Royal faction who were jockeying for power. The changes that the King proposed would have severely limited the power of both the nobles and the King, himself[119].

The unrest began as early as 1778, when the Grand Orient Masonic Lodges of France, under the leadership of the Illuminati and Adam Weishaupt, began to plot and plan for the revolution. Weishaupt had long been rumored to be funded by Rothschild and it did seem that his moves were well financed. As far as anyone could figure out at the time, the plan seemed to be for the revolution to sweep away the monarchy and bring on a general state of war in Europe with Rothschild financing all sides.

Of course, Rothschild, assuming that he was really the mastermind behind the Revolution, was not pinning all his hopes on the Masonic Lodges. His agents organized several other parties, such as the Royalist-anti reformists; the pro Duke of Orleans faction; the Girondins, the Jacobins (named for Jacob Joseph and Jacob Isaacs, friends of Rothschild. The Jacobin Clubs were organized in France,

---

[119] Nicolov, Nicola M., THE WORLD CONSPIRACY, TOPS, 10170 S.W. Nimbus, Portland, OR 97223. 1990.

England, Germany Italy and many other countries.) the Montagnards, the Dantonists, the Sans Culottes and others[120]. It is interesting to note that the term Jacobin became a name for the "Old" Masonic Order and the backers of the "Pretender" to the British Throne.

What is the most bizarre of the entire matter was that at the very same time agitators were inciting the people against the King, the King was trying to institute the very reforms that the revolutionists wanted. Therefore, the French Revolution was totally unnecessary. There was absolutely no need for millions of innocent people to die. However, only under the chaotic conditions of civil war can millions of deaths be justified and an entire country be looted.

Naturally, besides conspirators, in order to have a successful revolution, money is required. Those behind the French Revolution had a large amount of ready cash, enough to import thugs and killers and keep them on a retainer. These funds allegedly came from the Rothschild Banks[121].

Many have doubted the involvement of the Rothschilds in the atrocity known as the French Revolution. However, there is fairly substantial proof available that in fact the Rothschilds were, if not actively behind the

---

[120] Ibid
[121] Ibid

conspirators, at least helped with their funding.

According to several sources, the Magician, Cagliostro, was enrolled in Germany in the late 1700's as a member of the Illuminati. For several years, he acted as a recruiter and a messenger for the leadership of the Order. In 1790, Cagliostro was interrogated by the Holy See in Rome regarding his membership.

According to his testimony, during his initiation, Cagliostro was allowed to examine papers that stated the aims of the Illuminati was to overthrow thrones and altars and that the first throne attacked would be that of France. The second attack would be against Rome, itself.

As to the funding of this monstrous conspiracy, Cagliostro found out, from his Initiators, that the secret society possessed a large sum of money dispersed in banks in Amsterdam, Rotterdam, London, Genoa and Venice[122]. At this period of time, only the Rothschilds had the organization and network necessary to handle such a large mass of funds for such a clandestine operation.

THE ROLE OF SECRET SOCIETIES

There have been many stories regarding the

---

[122] Webster, Nesta H., <u>WORLD REVOLUTION,</u> Constable & Co. LTD., London. 1921.

involvement of many different secret societies in the French Revolution. I am sure that all of us have heard the story of the man who jumped onto the Guillotine when King Louis XVI's head fell into the basket, dipped his finger into the Royal Blood and yelled to the crowd "Jacques DeMolay, *thou art avenged.*"

Assuming the story to be true, the gentleman was of course referring to the suppression of the Knights Templar by the French throne. Jacques DeMolay had been the last known Grand Master of the Knights Templar. Phillipe the Fair of France had coveted the treasures of the Templars and, with the agreement of the Pope, he moved to arrest the Knights and seize their treasures.

To everyone's amazement, the treasure was missing and most of the Knights were gone. There were always rumors that the Knights of the Temple had merely gone underground rather than disbanding. It is known that the Templar fleet and most of the treasure of the Temple vanished from France and have never been seen since[123].

It may well be true that they had a hand in the overthrow of the Royal line. What is known is that the Knights Templar had pioneered the banking trade, actually

---

[123] Baigent, Michael and Richard Leigh, THE TEMPLE AND THE LODGE, Arcade Publishing. New York. 1989.

issuing a form of bank draft that could be obtained at one "Temple" and cashed at another. Allegedly, they were the first of the International Bankers.

A REVOLT OF THE COMMON PEOPLE

History records and teaches us that the French Revolution was one of the few times in history when the government was so despotic that the common man took to the streets to change things for the better. However, as we have seen above, this was just not so. True the masses did rise up in revolt, but at foreign instigation.

Rather than besmirch the names of agents of the conspiracy, those who write of this period try and place the blame for such things as the Reign of Terror on the frustration of the oppressed masses. However, the actual truth is that the majority of the most bloodthirsty of the "common people" were actually little better than cut throats and killers of the lowest social class. Their targets for "Madame Guillotine" was anyone who they had a grudge against, no matter how insignificant. The true "victims" of this revolt, besides the nobility, was the middle class, the backbone of French Society.

So thoroughly was the middle class decimated that most skilled trades in France were hard to fill. Many services were almost non-existent until new people could be trained. Some victims were chosen for death simply because someone thought that they were obviously "high born" and turned them in as enemies of the Revolution.

What most students of history have missed is that this alleged movement of the people was shrewdly manipulated by an inner circle made up of some of the very elements that the revolution was supposedly aimed at overthrowing, members of the Nobility. In fact, records have shown that one of the prime movers behind the uprising was Louis Philippe, the Duke of Orleans, cousin to the King[124]. The Duke recruited Mirabeau, a talented speaker, and spent a fortune recruiting agents to incite the masses. In fact, it was the Duke of Orleans' agents that caused the food shortages in Paris that was one of the main causes of the revolt.

Once the government had fallen, it was this small clique of leaders that actually made all of the decisions. The National Assembly was merely a rubber stamp for this group. That is until the inner circle had a falling out among themselves and then the leadership began to die as well.

There has been much written, both pro and con, regarding the involvement of the Masonic Orders in the

---

[124] Nicolov, Nicola M., THE WORLD CONSPIRACY, TOPS, 10170 S.W. Nimbus, Portland, OR 97223. 1990.

instigation of the Revolution. I would think that it is hard to miss the involvement of the more common secret societies such as the Masonic Orders in the Revolution since the very slogan of the Revolutionaries, "Liberty, Equality, and Fraternity[125]" was from Masonic teachings. However, some people see only what they want to see.

It is most interesting to note that even Robespierre, one of the most powerful men in Revolutionary France, claimed before the Assembly on June 26, 1794 (in his last speech) that:

"I don't trust all of these foreigners whose faces are covered with patriotic masks and who try to appear better Republicans than we are. These agents of foreign powers must be destroyed.[126]"

For his daring at pointing the finger at his true masters, Robespierre, himself, was sent to die in the public square. Like many others raised to the heights of power by the Conspiracy, he had dared to think himself too powerful to be removed. He was wrong.

THE SUN NEVER SETS ON THE BRITISH EMPIRE

There has been a great deal of information circulated

---

[125] Webster, Nesta H., THE FRENCH REVOLUTION. publisher unknown.
[126] Nicolov, Nicola M., THE WORLD CONSPIRACY, TOPS, 10170 S.W. Nimbus, Portland, OR 97223. 1990.

regarding the Conspiracy that allegedly has its' headquarters in the City controlling the British Government. There are numerous writings that tell of the power and control wielded by the rulers of this one mile square enclave. If these stories are true, then it would seem that there would be some evidence that British foreign policy would seem to favor the International Bankers. Amazingly enough, it seems that there is such evidence.

It would seem that since the rise to power of the Rothschild Clan in controlling the finances of Britain, that every major war has seen the total destruction of the "enemy". This has led to the "reconstruction" of the defeated country's economy by loans from the International Bankers and resulted in the creations of new power blocks that have resulted in ever larger profits for the Eternal Conspiracy.

The first, and the most overwhelming evidence of British Government assistance to and domination by the International Bankers, and the major rise in Rothschild fortunes, is found during the Napoleonic Wars. The payrolls for the British troops serving on the Continent were difficult to get to their destination until it was decided that the House of Rothschild should handle the payments through their French Offices. By the end of the war, the House of Rothschild had firm control of British finances and was the official banker of the British Government.

The most interesting part of this entire scenario is that there is much evidence that Napoleon received support and funding for his wars from the French Branch of the House of Rothschild. After the death of his father, Napoleon was in dire financial straits. According to history, Talleyrand introduced the young Napoleon to Amschel Rothschild who was looking for a protégé.

Rothschild desired a leader who would carry out his wishes and plans to weaken the Catholic Church and keep Europe in a constant state of War. Accordingly, he ordered his banks to finance and protect the young man. Napoleon used this protection and funding until he became Emperor. It was only when Napoleon turned on his Masters, by trying to put the welfare of his subjects first, that he was brought down into ruin by the very man who had raised him to power. It only cost millions of lives and millions of dollars to do the job.

Britain dedicated over two decades to trying to bring down Napoleon. Even so, in spite of the fact that the rest of Europe was united against him, Napoleon would probably not have been defeated at Waterloo had he not become ill and Marshall Soult been placed in command of the French forces. Marshall Soult was a relative, a cousin, I believe, of the

Rothschild Family.

BRITISH MILITARY FORCE

As an example of the pro-war stance of the British Government, let us first examine the modern cyclical wars that were conducted by Britain and her allies during the period from 1793 to 1918, then we will look at the wars conducted by the "Allies", as the post imperialist period has become to be known. Most of the cyclical wars were entered into in order to preserve or control the shifting balance of power; however, some were actually wars of imperialistic expansion. The listing of these modern cyclical wars is below[127]. Those cyclical wars that are considered of major historical importance are so indicated. Also indicated are those that were actually wars of imperialistic expansion.

Cyclical Wars

1. Napoleonic War - 1793-1815
    England, Prussia, Sweden, Russia and Austria vs. France

---

[127] Knuth, E.C., THE EMPIRE OF THE CITY, The Noontide Press, P.O. Box 1248, Torrance, CA 90505. 1983.

2. Turkish War   - 1827-1829
   England, France and Russia vs. Turkey and Egypt

3. Crimean War   - 1853-1856
   England, France, Turkey and Sardinia vs. Russia

4. American Civil War - 1861-1865 (Considered pivotal)
   England, France, Spain and the Confederate States of America vs. Russia and the United States

5. Franco-Prussian - 1870-1871 (Considered pivotal)
   France, England and Austria-Hungary vs. Germany, Russia and Italy

6. Russian-Turkish - 1877-1878
   Turkey, England, France and Austro-Hungary vs Russia and Germany

7. Egyptian War - 1882-1885 (Imperialistic Expansion)
   England, France and Austro-Hungary vs Egypt, Turkey and Russia

8. Spanish American - 1898-1899

United States and England vs Spain and Germany

9. Sudan War - 1898-1899 (Imperialistic Expansion)
England vs Sudanese-Egyptian Nationalists

10. Boer War - 1899-1902 (Imperialistic Expansion)
England vs Orange Free State and South African Rep.

11. Partition of Siam - 1899-1909 (Imperialistic Expansion)
England and France vs Siamese Nationalists

12. Russian-Japanese - 1904-1905 (Pivotal)
Japan and England vs Russia and Germany

13. Morocco Conflict - 1904-1906 (Imperialistic Expansion)
"The Allies" and Italy vs Germany and Austro-Hungary

14. Persian Conflict - 1907-1912 (Imperialistic Expansion)
England and France vs Russia and Germany

15. Morocco "Affair" - 1911   (Pivotal)
    England and France vs Germany

16. Tripoli War   - 1911-1912 (Pivotal)
    Italian reward or material quid for quo vs Turkey

17. 1st Balkan War - 1912-1913 (Pivotal)
    Greece, Serbia, Bulgaria and Montenegro vs. Turkey

18. 2nd Balkan War - 1913   (Pivotal)
    Rumania, Greece and Serbia vs Bulgaria

19. World War I   - 1914-1918
    "The Allies" and Italy, Rumania, Greece, Serbia, Montenegro and others vs. Germany, Austro-Hungary, Turkey and Bulgaria.

CHAPTER ELEVEN
THE PLAN CONTINUES

In the first book in this series[128], I discussed the evidence that the Conspiracy may be using a type of germ warfare as part of its programs. Additionally, there is evidence that this germ warfare program may be being conducted against certain racial or sexually oriented groups. I discussed the research of Dr. William Campbell Douglass and others in laying out a scenario that would substantiate my theory.

As you might recall, Dr. Douglass stated that AIDS had been created at Fort Detrick, Maryland and then used to contaminate the small pox vaccination program of the World Health Organization. I was amazed with the number of responses that I received to this particular chapter in the earlier book. This caused me to delve further into the question of whether or not there was a solid basis to the

---

[128] Hudnall, Ken, THE OCCULT CONNECTION, Omega, Anaheim, CA 92812.

theory that AIDS and other diseases may have been intentionally created by scientists.

There have been advanced two alleged reasons for such a deadly program being carried out. The first was that it was part of a germ warfare attack on the free world by the Communist nations. As proof of this allegation, researchers pointed to the fact that many loyal Communist Scientists were involved in the research at Fort Detrick, Maryland, the alleged starting point for the AIDS virus. The other scenario and the one to which I attach credence is that AIDS and other deadly viruses have been created at the orders of the Conspiracy and are being used to selectively eliminate segments of society that do not fit in with the master plan devised by the hidden Masters.

My scenario would explain why these germ warfare programs are so wide spread. For example, the continent of Africa has untold riches in mineral deposits, but the political situation and the local inhabitants make it impossible to openly mine these riches. However, if for some reason all or most of the local inhabitants died or were forced to move away or were too ill to oppose a takeover, then these riches could be mined in peace and quiet. The owners of these mining operations would become wealthy overnight. I would suggest that this is a major incentive for anyone with the resources to do so to create a virus to decimate the populations of undeveloped countries.

MAGIC

In our modern world, technology has reached a point where we can actually work what our ancestors would call magic. Unfortunately, so much of this super technology has been subverted to serve the purpose of those who would dominate and enslave us. A case in point is the almost pathological fear that most third world countries have regarding our main intelligence organization, the world famous, or is it infamous, Central Intelligence Agency (C.I.A.).

Most of us, if we give it any thought at all, shrug off the rumors regarding C.I.A. atrocities. After all, we are the good guys, how can we be doing the things that have alienated a good third of the world.

THE CENTRAL INTELLIGENCE AGENCY (C.I.A.)

The Central Intelligence Agency was created from the Office of Strategic Services (OSS) of World War II fame. It had been decided that in the post-World War II world that America needed a good intelligence service. Originally, its' mandate was to gather information from foreign countries and turn this information over to experts to study. Unfortunately, when powerful people are allowed to work in darkness and secrecy, they tend to procure additional power.

As a very real example of what uncontrolled power can do when coupled with immoral medical experiments, it is known that in the 1950's, Allan Dulles, then Director of the C.I.A., and a member of the Council on Foreign Relations (CFR) and a Rockefeller crony, backed a program involving strange, experimental medical procedures and mind control. In and of itself, he probably had the authority to authorize such a program, but he went one step beyond, he authorized a program to be developed that could control people against their will. In other words, he was looking for a way to enslave the minds of others.

This unauthorized program was carried out in Canada in order to try and limit leaks and bothersome exposure to potential media problems. In these Canadian experiments, the C.I.A. backed the work of Dr. Donald Ewen Cameron, a world famous psychiatrist who developed a technique he called depatterning, or destroying one's personality through electro-shock, drugs and surgery[129].

As a perfect example of what can happen when

---

[129] Thomas, Gordon, JOURNEY INTO MADNESS, Bantam Books. N.Y. 1989.

immoral men are given unlimited power, Dr. Cameron, with C.I.A. knowledge and support, trained some of the most infamous "torturers" known in the world today. It was one of these "medical men" trained by Dr. Cameron that worked on the C.I.A.'s own William Buckley, station chief in Beirut, Lebanon who was kidnapped and broken by terrorists[130].

It is acts such as these that have caused rumors to run rampant throughout the world that the C.I.A. is behind almost every evil from acid rain in the Far East to the famine in Ethiopia. It would be laughable if it were not for the fact that it has turned out that our C.I.A. has, in fact been behind much evil in the third world countries. As if this weren't bad enough, there are even stories leaked to the media that our own C.I.A. may be responsible for one of the most deadly diseases of our time, AIDS.

Is this rumor true? Is a branch of our own government in the business of wiping out entire segments of the human race? There are many who believe that the CIA may have created the AIDS virus to wipe out the gay population or perhaps to depopulate the continent of Africa. Of course, the C.I.A. has been a Third World whipping boy for years.

It was to prove or disprove this theory that started me on my research into the question of whether or not the CIA,

---

[130] Ibid

or any other U.S. Government Agency, for that matter, might have created the AIDS virus. I wouldn't have been surprised to discover that the answer to the question was in the affirmative, but the preliminary results of my research shows that while it probably wasn't the C.I.A., as an organization, that is, that created AIDS, there is a great deal of data that does make it look like this deadly disease was created in the laboratory and was not a natural occurrence.

During the course of my research, I came across an unbelievable number of articles, newsletters and books that dealt with some of the little known information regarding the origins of the AIDS virus. Most of these documents contained information that tended to discredit the official position as espoused by the Center for Disease Control (CDC).

To make matters even worse, I found some information that made it appear that there might even be a conspiracy to keep the American Public mis-informed. According to a Dr. Robert G. Grant, "there is a conspiracy of silence although at times it seems more to resemble a campaign of dis-information with clear political overtones[131]." This is a very strange approach to so deadly a

---

[131] Grant, Dr. Robert G, "Emergency Disease alert AIDS," American Christian Voice, Box 37053, Washington, D.C.

disease. Why would government organization charged with combatting AIDS put out disinformation about that disease that would tend to confuse the population and disrupt programs designed to stop the disease?

One of the most fascinating of the newsletters that I found was a copy of a newsletter called **THE BULLETIN OF THE COMMITTEE TO RESTORE THE CONSTITUTION**[132] that is dated March, 1988. In this newsletter is a reprint of an article by Dr. William Campbell Douglass M.D. entitled "WHO MURDERED AFRICA". This was not intended to be a rhetorical question for according to Dr. Douglass, the WHO stands for the World Health Organization.

This article, discussed below, originally appeared in the September, 1987 issue of **THE CUTTING EDGE**[133] Dr. William Campbell Douglass, publisher. This magazine is a continuing update on the AIDS epidemic. This article was also the basis for a chapter of my earlier book.

THE WORLD HEALTH ORGANIZATION

For those who are not aware of the existence of the

---

[132] Roberts, Archibald E. LT COL., AUS, ret. Director, P.O. Box 986, Ft. Collins, CO 80522. (303) 484 2575
[133] THE CUTTING EDGE: Douglass, Dr. William Campbell M.D., 2470 Windy Hill Rd., Suite 440, Marietta, GA 30067

World Health Organization, it is a creation of the United Nations. Allegedly, the World Health Organization was originally intended to combat diseases on a worldwide basis; unfortunately, it has become, according to many, merely a propaganda tool for Eastern Bloc Countries. However, now it is necessary to ask, is the World Health Organization (WHO) responsible for the spread of the AIDS virus? Dr. William Douglass makes it quite clear that, as a result of his research, he believes that the World Health Organization has been responsible for millions of deaths in Africa. These deaths were not caused directly, of course, but, instead were done through the use of the AIDS virus.

Such an accusation is bad enough, but to make matter even worse, he goes on to say, we have all had our lives endangered by this disease. In other words, he throws out the concept of the "dangerous classifications" and takes the position that we are all in danger from this killer disease.

As Dr. Douglass correctly points out, AIDS is a virus, and like all types of virus, by its' very nature, it can be passed on to others. This would seem to make it appear that the CDC's position that AIDS can only be passed by "close" sexual contact or sharing a dirty needle.

As Dr. Douglass also so correctly points out, a common cold is a virus, just like AIDS is a virus. We have all, at one time or another had a common cold. We have all caught colds and not known how we caught them. We have also all been around a friend who has a virus and later come down with the virus ourselves. Consider the implications of what would have happened if the common cold was as deadly as AIDS.

SEX

In the area of sex, there has been much talk regarding the passing of AIDS and other virus' through "unsafe sex". In fact even as I write this, there is news that a famous Basketball Star has discovered that he has been exposed to AIDS. He apparently was infected through having sex with someone who was infected. So this makes one ask what is considered as "safe sex".

In regard to this question, the CDC as well as other "responsible agencies" have taken the position that using a condom will lessen the chances of getting AIDS from sex. However, according to the research of Gene Antonio in his book, The AIDS COVER-UP, women who use condoms have a 400% greater risk factor and women using birth control pills, have a 350% greater risk factor[134]. According

---

[134] Antonio, Gene, The AIDS Cover up, Ignatius Press, San Francisco, 1987.

the Dr. J. Nicholas Gordon, M.D. only abstinence before marriage and mutually monogamous sex afterwards are the best methods of preventing sexually transmitted AIDS[135]. However, when Dan Quayle, Vice-President of the United States made this same comment, he was ridiculed by the press.

THE ORIGINS OF AIDS

There has been much wild speculation regarding the origin or the AIDS virus, but Dr. Douglass very analytically looks at the suspects that have been named as the main carriers of aids, the homosexuals, the green monkey and the Haitians, to name a few. These so called carriers, he insists were only pawns in what he describes as a viricidal attack on the non-Communist world. For Dr. Douglass, like so many others, seems to see AIDS as a form of biological warfare, as it may well be.

Dr. Douglass states that if you believe the government propaganda that AIDS is hard to catch, i.e. can only be caught through close sexual contact and sharing infected needles, then you are going to die even sooner than the rest of us.

---

[135] Gordon, J. Nicholas, M.D., Director of Student Health Services, Ga. Tech., Atlanta, GA. "Information About AIDS."

To demonstrate what he is saying regarding the risk involved with virus', Dr. Douglass points to yellow fever, which is also a virus in order to show that no direct contact whatsoever is necessary to catch some virus' from infected people. This virus can be caught from the bite of a certain type of mosquito. Malaria is a parasite also carried also by mosquitos, a parasite that in the last century was quite deadly to infected humans.

ANOTHER CARRIER

The malaria parasite is many times larger than the AIDS virus (like comparing a pinhead to a moose head) yet the mosquito easily carries this relatively large organism to man. It is only recently, after several Physicians raised the question, that our government has had to admit that AIDS can be passed by at least one type of mosquitos, the Asian Tiger Mosquito, to be specific. This particular type of mosquito has been recently *introduced* into the U.S. and is found predominately in the Southeast section of our country (i.e. Georgia, Florida and Alabama).

To show the dangers of this mosquito carrier, one has to only look to the Florida town of Belle Glade to see what can happen when the Asian Tiger Mosquito has free rein to pass the disease. The Tropical Disease Center, located in

Florida has studied the disease spread in this town and concluded that the Asian Tiger Mosquito was the most important vector in the spread of the disease in this tiny town. The percentage of AIDS cases in that town is astronomical in comparison with the rest of the country.

Dr. Douglass also points to the example of the tuberculosis germ which can live outside the body and be passed to uninfected people who handled the effects of those already infected. The infection process is possible due to the fact that the tuberculosis germ can survive for a time outside the body and still be deadly. Infection of new victims is possible as long as the germ is alive. Well, new studies show that AIDS virus can survive for a period of from ten to fifteen days outside the human body. This would mean that sheets stained with the body fluids of AIDS patients can actually infect new victims for ten to fifteen days, in the same manner as the tuberculosis germ.

Viruses grow in both animals and humans. Fortunately, for us, most animal viruses do not affect humans. However, there are a few major, and deadly, exceptions such as yellow fever, smallpox and plague. Other animal viruses effect just the infected animal and are not passed to other animals or to man, such as bovine leukemia found in cattle and another virus found in sheep called sheep visna virus. Both of these viruses cause a very lethal form of cancer.

It is also to these viruses that we have to look for the beginnings of the AIDS virus, for the AIDS virus is a very unusual type of virus. To understand what the AIDS disease is, you actually have to look at the animal world and viruses that in their natural state do not and cannot be passed to humans. Specifically you have to look at the two animal diseases mentioned above, one that effects cows called the bovine leukemia virus (BLV) and the other being a disease that occurs in sheep called sheep visna virus.

These two diseases have something in common; the common factor is that they are called "retro viruses", meaning that these viruses' can change the genetic composition of the cells that they invade. Sounds a little bit like AIDS doesn't it?

Dr. Douglass found evidence that the World Health Organization asked for the creation of an AIDs like virus in its' publications[136].Specifically he points to such statements as "An attempt should be made to see if viruses can in fact exert selective effects on immune functions. The possibility should be looked into that the immune response to the virus

---

[136] Allison, et al. Bull, WHO 1972, 47:257 63 and Amos, et. al. Federal Procedures. 1972, 31:1087:$IAIDS:; Requested By the World Health Organization:

itself may be impaired if the infecting virus damages, more or less selectively, the cell responding to the virus."

It is interesting to note that it is sheer insanity to think that anyone would possibly want to develop such a disease for, as Dr. Douglass correctly points out, if you destroy the immune system, you destroy the man. It is at this point that both this author and Dr. Douglass asked the same question "Is it even remotely possible that the World Health Organization would want to develop a virus that would wipe out the human race?"

Of course, it is possible to find a rational explanation for the original research in this area. It would appear that scientists were looking for a way to suppress the immune system in specific areas for use in organ transplants. One of the main causes of death in organ transplant recipients is rejection of the new organ by the body. A method of reducing the immune response would save thousands of lives. However, what was developed was a virus that seems to completely destroy the immune system.

I know what some of you are thinking at this point. You are remembering all of the great scientists, as well as the various medical groups who have publicly stated that AIDS was caused by the African green monkey biting a native, who in turn passed the disease on to others.

There is only one fatal flaw in this theory, there has been no proof that AIDS occurs naturally in any animal. This being the case, then how did the Green Monkey get the disease, assuming, of course, that he ever had it in the first place?

(**Authors Note:** *Since this was first written, I have discovered that the Green Monkey has had an AIDS type virus for as long as man has known about the Green Monkey, however, the Green Monkey is not harmed by the virus. Nor is there any evidence whatsoever that can show that the Green Monkey pass this virus to man.)*

It should also be noted that AIDS seemed to spring up almost simultaneously in the United States, Haiti, Brazil and Central Africa. This virus sprang up almost simultaneously even though it can have from a five to twenty year incubation period. Therefore, in order to spring up simultaneously in several areas of the world, it had to have started independently in those same areas of the world. Dr. Douglass points out that it is not even genetically possible for the bite of the Green Monkey to pass the disease to man. So much for that "official" theory.

Dr. Douglass quotes the research work of a Dr. Theodore Strecker, who is alleged to have found proof that the National Cancer Institute in collaboration with the World Health Organization actually made the AIDS virus in their labs at Fort Detrick, Maryland (now part of the National Cancer Institute). He further states that AIDS was created by combining two retro viruses, bovine leukemia and sheep visna virus. Then the combination was injected into human tissue cultures and allowed to mutate. This procedure created the very first human retro virus, one that has shown itself to be almost one hundred percent deadly.

(**Authors Note:** *There seems to be some confusion on the point of Dr. Theodore Strecker. There are actually two people, brothers, named Strecker. Dr. Robert Strecker, a medical doctor practicing in Los Angeles, CA. and Theodore Strecker, an attorney practicing in St. Louis, MO. Theodore Strecker was heavily involved in disseminating the AIDS research conducted by his brother and other researchers.*
One evening Theodore Strecker was found dead, with a .22 caliber hole <u>in the back of his head.</u> The death was classified a suicide. Rumor has it that research material in his possession was missing when the body was discovered.)

Now let's get to the good part, or the bad part depending on your point of view. According to Dr. Douglass, and confirmed in other research I have conducted, the U.S. Government invited doctors from around the world, to include many from the Communist Bloc to participate in the anti-cancer research going on at Ft. Detrick. This was part of Richard Nixon's war on Cancer. This program was also confirmed by Carlton Gajdusek, Chief of the National Institute of Health's Laboratory of Central Nervous System Studies and also the Laboratory of Slow, Latent and Temperate Virus Infections[137].

Mr. Gajdusek is quoted in an article in the March, 1986 issue of Omni magazine (page 106) as saying, in response to a question as to whether or not Ft. Detrick was a biological warfare center, that:

> "No, emphatically no! There is no defensive or offensive warfare microbiology done at Ft. Detrick today. It is the national cancer research facility of the NIH. In this facility (referring to the research facilities at Ft. Detrick) I have a building where more good and loyal communist scientists from the USSR and mainland China work-- with full passkeys to all the laboratories-- than there are Americans. With night working U.S. citizens and foreign Communist investigators here, obviously there is no "secret" bacterial warfare going on. Even the Army's Infectious Disease Unit (a euphemistic name for the Army's Germ Warfare Unit) is loaded with foreign workers not always friendly nationals. It is a valid basic research unit on

---

[137] Omni Magazine, March issue, 1986. page 106.

worldwide problems of infectious diseases in which no classified or secret activities unfold."

(Author's Question: Isn't this kind of like hiring the burglar to guard your valuables?).

In the 1972 issue of a document called the <u>Federal Proceedings of the United States</u>, representatives of the World Health Organization said:

"In the relation to the immune response a number of useful experimental approaches can be visualized". This same spokesman went on to say that a good way to test this disease would be to put it into a vaccination program, then wait for the results. It was felt that very good statistical data would come out of the study of "sibship", or injecting brothers and sisters at the same time and seeing who dies first. (Author's Comment: Kind of chokes you up, knowing that you might be a part of a WHO Study, doesn't it.)

Dr. Douglass contends, as do many others, that the World Health Organization's smallpox vaccination program conducted in Uganda and other central African states, Haiti, Brazil and Japan in 1972 was used to test this new killer virus. The epidemiology results from these countries confirm that this had to be the manner in which the disease spread.

Are you prepared to dismiss these finding as the opinion of simply one Physician? Well, let's look further. In the January 11, 1986 issue of Lancet[138], Dr. R.J. Biggars stated that "The AIDS agent . . .could not have originated de novo." Now we have a serious medical journal questioning the "Green Monkey Theory". A good start toward proving my point, but is it possible that Dr. Douglass is simply paranoid and seeing a pattern where it does not exist?

In Easy Reader, Jon Rappaport wrote about an interview he conducted with Robert Matthews, technical correspondent of the London Times[139]. In this interview, Mr. Matthews, told Mr. Rappaport that the World Health Organization, itself, had suspected that its smallpox immunization program might have some connection with the rapid outbreak and spreading of the AIDS virus. As a result, an outside consultant was hired to perform an independent study and the study confirmed the connection. The WHO quickly buried the report[140].

It is quite possible that the World Health Organization was totally innocent and its facilities were used by renegade physicians who were actually members of the

---

[138] Lancet, January 11, 1986
[139] Rappoport, Jon, "News Blackout on Pox Vaccine Link to AIDS Protecting WHO? Easy Reader, June 4, 1987, p. 12.
[140] Ibid

Conspiracy. Unfortunately, when it appears to have discovered that it was used by a person or persons unknown, the World Health Organization acted in a manner designed to assist the true culprits in escaping. It covered up what had happened.

Unfortunately, for the human race, this was not, and is not, the only cover-up going on. The United States medical community has had a cover-up of its own going on. This was in regard to an even more blatant attempt to "infect" the American people. As we will see in the next chapter, we may all have a "time bomb" ticking away in our vein

CHAPTER TWELVE

A TRAGIC MEDICAL COVER-UP

"Despite cases in which smallpox vaccination plainly failed to protect the population, and despite the rampant side-effects of the methods, the proponents of vaccination continued their attempts to justify the methods by claims that the disease had declined in Europe as a whole during the period of its compulsory use. If the decline could be correlated with the use of the vaccination, then all else could be set aside, and the advantage between its current low incidence could be shown to outweigh the periodic failures of the method, and to favor the continued use of vaccination. However, the credit for the decline in the incidence of smallpox could not be given to vaccination. The fact it that its incidence declined in all parts of Europe whether or not vaccination was employed."
Leon Chaitow, **_Vaccination and Immunization_**.

Is it true, was the black death of the twentieth century, called AIDS, created by scientists and intentionally spread around the world? Is it even remotely possible that immunization programs designed to eradicate ancient diseases that have plagued mankind have also spread an even more dangerous killer?

Dr. Eva Lee Snead, M.D. of San Antonio, Texas has also determined that there is a connection between the AIDS virus and governmental sponsored immunization programs. To begin her research, Dr. Snead started with several questions on her mind:

1. How did AIDS start?

2. If AIDS doubles every 14 months (this was the rate at the time of her article) that would total only several thousand cases since 1977 (the first reported official AIDS case). How did the number of cases come to numbered in the millions?

3. Why does AIDS affect primarily those in their late 30's? With the incubation period being anywhere from 20 to 30 years (this data may or may not be still valid), what happened 20 to 30 years ago that could have infected them?

Dr. Snead looked at the fact that the polio vaccine immunization program was begun about thirty years ago and administered to millions of people. This particular immunization program was directed at children, many of whom are now in their late thirties. Is this significant since the average age of the population that seems to be effected the most strongly by AIDS is in their late thirties[141]?

A COVER-UP?

It is most interesting to note that Dr. Snead obtained much of her information from the Food and Drug Administration (FDA) through the Freedom of Information Act. The data she received went back thirty years, and showed that the FDA had known about the contamination of the vaccines for several years. It is very unnerving to be made aware that at the same time the Government, and most physicians, were crowing about the benefits of having your children vaccinated (if you are old enough to remember, vaccinations were made mandatory for public school attendance) that the medical community was aware that there were severe and potentially deadly problems with the vaccination program.

In fact, in 1960, even before the start of the high profile polio inoculation program, the World Health

---

[141]Snead, Eva Lee, M.D., "AIDS: Immunization Related Syndrome," Health Freedom News, Monrovia, CA., July, 1987

Organization (WHO) issued a bulletin informing the medical community that undesirable viruses were being found in the very vaccines that were being used to inoculate American school children. In 1963, "Science Digest", the Journal of the New York Academy of Sciences reported that humans are susceptible to simian tumor virus. "Science Digest" also reported the "near disaster" of the polio immunization program[142]. So why was no one outside of the medical community and the FDA told about this monstrous screw-up?

POLIO

Just like the World Health Organization's smallpox immunization program, the American polio immunization program was also exported to Africa, Haiti, Brazil and many other third world countries. Is this a pattern? Are potentially deadly programs developed in the advanced countries and then "tried out" in the third world countries?

Even if this is the case, it would seem that there are occasionally errors made in the program. Interestingly enough, in 1977, the Atlantic Monthly reported that millions of Americans had been contaminated with a disease called

---

[142] "Near Disaster with the Salk Vaccine." Science Digest, Dec. 1963.

SV-40[143]. No big deal, right? At least it wasn't AIDS.

Perhaps, however, researchers discovered some very unusual things about Simian Virus-40 (SV40). First, it is passed the same way as AIDS. The clinical findings in regard to SV-40 are identical to AIDS. So we have the Polio vaccination program contaminated with a virus that produces something identical to AIDS which also has the identical clinical symptoms. We could call SV-40 the swine flu, but it will still kill.

I remember that little dittie I heard in the Army: If it walks like a duck and quacks like a duck and looks like a duck, chances are it's a duck.

If a disease is passed like AIDS, has symptoms like AIDS and the clinical findings are identical to AIDS, then no matter what we call it, isn't it possible it's AIDS? For those of you who have not heard of SV-40 before, read on.

---

[143] Bennett, William and Joel, Gurin, "Science That Frightens Scientists," Atlantic Monthly, Feb. 1977 - Excerpt from a Letter from Lynn M. Draft, White House Policy Staff, to Dick Gregory, April 11, 1977. Quoting: "It is true that the SV40 virus was discovered in the early 1960's. It is also true that the virus was found in certain viral vaccines prepared from virus pools grown in monkey kidney cell cultures. However, the virus had not been recognized as a contaminant prior to that time, although millions of people have received the vaccine during the 1950's" ". . .contamination of the vaccine was unintentional due to lack of knowledge."

SIMIAN VIRUS 40 AND THE POLIO VACCINE

AIDS is called HIV, (incidentally, there are now HIV 1 and HIV 2). However, another virus, some thirty years old caused almost the same clinical findings as AIDS, this was a virus called SIMIAN VIRUS 40 (SV-40), also suspected as being called by the African Green Monkey. This particular virus also causes birth defects, leukemia and many other forms of malignancy[144]. Additionally, the following symptoms of SV-40 and AIDS are similar:

a. **Interference of T-Cell Formation:** *The SV-40 cell cultures inhibit proliferation of T-cells and can be caused by direct inoculation or by contact with individuals who harbor the virus*[145].

b. **Development of Malignancies:** *SV-40 caused a large percentage of lab animals to develop malignancies*[146].

c. **Body Wasting:** *SV-40 causes a decrease in protein production, also a decrease of albumen, a sign of*

---

[144] Ibid
[145] Todaro, G.H., and Green, H., Virology, pages, 752 754, 1968.
[146] Snider, Arthur J., "Near Disaster with the SALK Vaccine," Science Digest, pages 40 41, Dec. 1963.

severe body wasting[147].

d. **Increased Birth Defects, Tumors, Leukemias:** *Results of the study indicated a high frequency of leukemia and human mongolism*[148].

Dr. Snead made an attempt to research SIMIAN VIRUS 40 in the medical literature and found that all reference to it stopped in 1964, as if it had never existed. However, she did discover some literature that discussed the fact that this virus may have contaminated the polio vaccine[149].

SV-40 is also a very unique virus in another way. It is a virus, and like AIDS, a virus is defined as any particle, natural or man-made, which can enter a cell and cause this cell to make copies of itself. Only the living cell has this reproduction power. SV-40 has the ability to carry information in a piggyback fashion into a cell. Research shows that this may be the part that SV-40 plays in the AIDS virus. It was felt by some researchers that SV-40 may predispose to secondary viral infection by destroying the

---

[147] Henry Ford Hospital Medical Journal, Vol. 15, summer 1963.
[148] "Proceedings of the National Academy of Sciences," p. 1170, July 1962
[149] Horwath, B.L. & Fornosi, F. Acta Microbiologica Hungary, Vol. 11, pages 271 275.

immune system. It is interesting to note that SV-40 was present, yet passed undetected, in the early stages of development of the Salk and Sabine polio vaccines[150].

A BINARY VIRUS?

As a result of the discovery of SV-40 a new theory has arisen. Is it possible that AIDS is a binary virus. In other words, is it possible that AIDS is actually two viruses that work together to kill. By this I mean is it possible that HIV by itself is not deadly? There are many whose blood show exposure to AIDS (due to the development of AIDS anti-bodies) but who do not have AIDS itself.

What I am purposing is that someone who already has been exposed to HIV also is exposed to SV-40, or some other activating mechanism, which combine to produce a truly deadly virus.

If this is correct, then as a result of the 1960's polio vaccination program, most Americans in their 30's have been exposed to SV-40. If one of those people is exposed to someone with HIV, then they will die. However, until that time, they walk around with that time bomb ticking away. Remember, SV-40 cannot be detected with most medical tests, however, HIV can be detected. So when one of those

---

[150] Ibid

with AIDS has tests, only the HIV show up, not the SV-40. In this manner, the binary nature of the virus is kept hidden.

Naturally, those of you with medical training are going to object to a non-medically trained individual such as myself advancing a theory in such an area. However, I would submit that at this time there is no proof that HIV is deadly or even gives rise to AIDS. As my proof I will point to data given in AIDS INC., the work by Jon Rappoport I have quoted from several times. According to Mr. Rappoport, depending on what study you read, HIV has been isolated in only 50-80% of those with full blown AIDS. This means that in 20-30% of those with full blown AIDS, HIV has not been present.

According to Koch's postulates, from every person with a given disease, remove the same germ in every case. Then inject this germ into animals and in every case, this should produce all of the symptoms of the original disease. Therefore, in every case of AIDS, extract the HIV "germ" and inject it into an animal. If your theory is correct, the animal should develop AIDS.

Unfortunately, this has not worked. As pointed out earlier, in 20-30% of the cases studied, the HIV virus has not even been present. Additionally, in a medical study conducted in the U.S. 100 chimps were injected with high concentrations of HIV. Two of the chimps immediately developed infected lymph glands. However, in thirty weeks the condition returned to normal. In the other ninety eight chimps, there were no AIDS symptoms at all. It has been over four years since some of these chimps were injected.

MORE PROOF

Additional proof of the connection between immunization programs and AIDS came from no less a source than the United States Army. A 19 year old recruit, in perfect health, after his in-processing small pox vaccination, developed AIDS and in a very short time died. This incident brought the matter to the attention of Walter Reed Army Hospital. However, in typical fashion, officials tried to hide the truth behind a wall of lies and suppositions.

Even though there was no proof that the recruit had ever been previously exposed to AIDS, it was decided that perhaps the vaccination program merely activated dormant AIDS. The Walter Reed Medical Team even submitted a paper to the New England Journal of Medicine reporting their discovery of the connection between vaccination programs and the possible stimulation of dormant AIDS disease.

Even the front page story of the London Times for

May 11, 1987[151] confirmed the fact that the AIDS virus was spread through the World Health Organization's smallpox vaccination program of 1972[152].

Quoted as their source for the story, which was written by Pearce Wright, Science Editor for the London Times, was an unnamed (he wished to keep his identity secret for fear of his job and his life) advisor to the World Health Organization, as well as, the Walter Reed Army Medical Center in Washington D.C.

However, in this story, the London times, conforming to party line, took the position that the small pox vaccination merely triggered dormant AIDS, instead of being the route of original infection. Of course, there is no medical evidence that there is such a thing as "dormant" AIDS, but it would seem to prove my theory that AIDS is a binary virus, where the vaccination might furnish the "activating" element to complete the required binary virus.

LOOK AT THE NUMBERS

If you get caught, lie, seems to be the position taken by the World Health Organization. However, if the reader isn't convinced yet regarding the culpability of the World

---

[151] London Times, Front Page Story, "Small Pox Vaccine Triggered Aids Virus", by Pearce Wright, Science Editor.
[152] AIDS:;Passed Through Smallpox Injection Programs:

Health Organization, let's look at the infection figures for the countries involved in the original small pox vaccination program.:

The seven African countries with the most reported cases of AIDS are also the seven countries with the most people given the smallpox vaccine in the World Health Organization's vaccination program. Those seven countries are,

- Zaire, with 36,878,000 people vaccinated;
- Zambia, with 19,060,000;
- Tanzania, with 14,972,000;
- Uganda, with 11,616,000;
- Malawi, with 8,118,000;
- Rwanda, with 3,382,000; and
- Burundi, with 3,274,000 people vaccinated.

Incidentally, Brazil, the only South American country covered by the vaccination program, also has the highest incidence of AIDS in South America.

According to Dr. Douglass, AIDS didn't exist in the U.S. before 1978. He feels that it was actually here but not triggered until later. It is known that the first officially diagnosed case of AIDS was reported in 1973. The patient was a Northern European female medical doctor who was working for a medical mission in Africa. Allegedly the first case of AIDS in this country was brought by a homosexual male flight attendant on an international flight from Africa.

However, Dr. Douglass maintains that it was another factor that triggered the AIDS virus in this country in 1978. He feels that this triggering mechanism was another government program. In his writings, Dr. Douglass submitted his theory that the disease was introduced or triggered in this country through the Hepatitis B vaccine program.

To prove his theory, Dr. Douglass points to a Doctor W. Schmugner, a Russian born and trained physician who came to this country in 1969. This Russian Doctor, in only a short time after his arrival in this country, became head of the New York City Blood Bank shortly before 1978. According to Dr. Douglass, for Dr. Schmugner to climb so high in the medical community so fast took behind the scenes assistance. This proposal brings us back to the Conspiracy.

According to Dr. Douglass it was allegedly Dr. Schmugner who set up the rules for the hepatitis vaccine studies. His guidelines called for it to be tested only on homosexual males between the ages of 20 and 40 who were not monogamous. Therefore, newspaper advertisements were taken out in the five cities where the testing was to be conducted. These advertisements called for homosexual male volunteers between the required ages.

In 1981, the Center for Disease Control (CDC) reported that four (4%) percent of those receiving the hepatitis vaccine were AIDS infected. In 1984, the CDC reported that sixty (60%) percent of those who received those vaccinations were now AIDS infected. Since 1984, the CDC has refused to give out anymore statistics on the program[153]. Rumor has it that the incidence of infection among those who took part in the vaccination study is now close to 100%.

Two things should be noted, the first is that Dr. Schmugner is now dead, therefore, we can't question him as to his motivation or his associations. The second is that the Hepatitis B vaccine tests were conducted in New York City, Los Angeles, San Francisco, Chicago and Miami, all cities with a large homosexual population and a growing AIDS population.

Because of the numerous genetic combinations possible with this virus (according to Dr. Douglass the number is 9,000 to the fourth power), there can never be a vaccine. After all, how can you develop a drug vaccine for a disease that simply changes its' molecular design to combat the vaccine? There are certain drug treatments that do seem to alleviate some of the worst effects of the AIDS virus, unfortunately,

---

[153] Data released by the Center for Disease Control..

most of these drug treatments have side effects that are as bad as or worse than the disease itself.

However, according the T. E. Bearden in his book AIDS--Biological Warfare, there is a cure, but medical science is refusing to accept it[154]. The author of this excellent book believes that this cure is ignored because it does not call for expensive drugs. In fact, this cure does not depend on drugs of any type which of course offends the drug companies. This cure depends on electromagnetism.

[I highly recommend that those of you interested in following up on this topic read the book called AIDS-Biological Warfare[155].]

I would not want to leave you with the idea that the World Health Organization set out to wipe out the human race. However, the evidence is fairly clear that it was the smallpox vaccination program that may have started or spread this dreaded disease. The why, we may never know and at this point, it really doesn't matter. What does matter is how do we stop the further spread of this killer disease?

It is possible that we may have created a monster in

---

[154] Lt. Col. (RET) T. E. Bearden, AIDS Biological Warfare, Tesla Book Company, P.O. Box 1649, Greenville, Texas 75401, 1988.
[155] Ibid

the name of research. Did a virus created from monkey cells in the 1960's, called SV-40 become introduced into the cultures from which the polio vaccine was created that we were given in the early 1960's. (I had this one myself.) If so, what do we do now?

BIOLOGICAL WARFARE

Before we leave this chapter, I think it only fair that we take one last look at the area of Biological Warfare (CBR or CBW). Is it possible that what we call AIDS is the result of chemical or biological attacks on certain groups of the population? Such an attack would make it easier for invaders to overwhelm sick or dying defenders. It could of course be justified in that many lives would be saved and the war shortened if the enemy simply died in their beds. For these and many other reasons more and more military leaders are authorizing the use of such weapons against their enemies. After all, enough plague germs to decimate a continent could be carried in test tube and created in a laboratory the size of an average kitchen without any special equipment.

As for who would use such weapons, according to a 1975 Fort Belvoir, VA publication entitled <u>Decontamination of Water Containing Chemical Warfare Agents</u>, "... *it is theoretically possible to develop so-called ethnic chemical weapons, which would be designed to exploit naturally occurring differences in vulnerability among specific population groups. Thus, such a weapon would be capable of incapacitating or killing a selected enemy population to a significantly greater extent than the population of friendly forces."*

Reported in a study called <u>A HIGHER FORM OF KILLING</u>, the comments of a Dr. Leonard MacArthur before a 1969 House Appropriations Committee are interesting. In a discussion of budget funds for defense for 1970, Dr. MacArthur made the following statements:

"Within the next 5 to 10 years, it would probably be possible to make a new infective microorganism which would differ in certain important respects from any known disease-causing organisms. Most important of these is that it might be refractory to the immunological and therapeutic processes upon which we depend to maintain our relative freedom from infectious disease."

CHAPTER THIRTEEN

AND SO?

It goes without saying that the President of the United States is elected to serve and protect all of the people. However, the evidence that I have presented in this book clearly points to actions taken by our government that are not in our best interest and in fact which gave aid and comfort to those who would destroy our way of life..

In the case of President Barack Hussein Obama, we see actions taken by our government that are clearly totally contrary to our best interest as a country and he still has the support of 40% of the American people. It just doesn't make sense. Almost since the day he entered office, he has been a controversial and divisive president.

As our first Black President, Obama has been very quick to play the race card whenever someone opposes his or his policies. Actually, that is not exactly true, rather his staff screams out the race card while he just smiles his campaign smile.

As I write these words, our great President, who has claimed he is too big for the Presidency and who promised the most transparent administration in history is juggling several lies and secrets that will devastate this country. It is the plan of our Commander in Chief to reduce the size of our military at the same time he gets us into one war after another. He is also getting ready to admit up to 34,000,000 illegal aliens into this country who the Democratic Party believes will vote Democrat for generations.

As if this is not enough, he is opening our borders to anyone who wants to come. As of this past summer tens of thousands of illegal immigrant children have swarmed across our southern border bringing diseases to which we have no immunity. Instead of dealing with these illnesses, he has ordered that the illegals be secretly carried to temporary facilities across the country.

Rules that the rest of us must obey are being waived for these illegals who came here in their thousands as a result of campaigns secretly run by our government in various South American countries. It can be said that no one could be this inept by sheer accident. What he is doing is part of a long term program to devastate this country politically, financially and medically.

Since his election, he has shoveled the cash out of the Treasury to the banks and other supporters and devastated the economy. Could such a series of problems be anything other than a well thought out plan?

HOPEFULLY NOT THE END!

INDEX

1
1st Balkan War, 215

2
2nd Balkan War, 215

3
300, 75, 79, 104

A
Adam, 31, 36, 37, 38, 61, 82, 154, 155, 157
Adept, 83
AIDS, 217, 218, 221, 222, 223, 224, 225, 226, 227, 228, 229, 231, 232, 235, 237, 238, 239, 241, 242, 243, 244, 245, 246, 247, 248, 249, 250, 251, 252
Akkadians, 29
Allied, 198
American Civil War, 186, 213
American Cyanamid, 199
American Home Products, 198
American Motors, 199
American Revolution, 130, 131, 141, 149, 150
Amsterdam Bourse, 175
Anaconda Copper, 198
Ancient Gods, 4, 20, 53, 81, 125
Ancient Mysteries, 80, 81, 82, 83
Angel of Death, 4
Annanaki, 26, 27, 29, 30, 32, 33, 34, 38, 40, 41, 42, 43, 44, 46, 50, 52, 78, 81, 84, 114
Aryan Nation, 67
Atlantic Richfield Oil, 197
Avon, 26, 29, 30, 32, 35, 38, 46, 48, 198

B
Baalbek, 27
Babylonians, 29
Bacon, Sir Francis, 137, 141
Bad-Tibira, 32
Bagehot, Walter, 167
Bailey, Alice, 66
Bank of England, 143, 144, 145, 146, 147, 168, 185
Baring Brothers & Co. Limited, 184
Bendix, 199
Boeing, 197
Boer War, 214
Bonnie, 13
Book of Enoch, 25, 27, 37, 39, 40, 43, 50
Book of Genesis, 30, 31
Borden, 198
Boston Tea Party, 150, 156
Bovine leukemia virus, 229
Braniff, 198
Brigade of Guards, 168
British Board of Trade, 147
Bruce, Robert, 134
Buckley, William, 221
Buderus, 175

C
C.I.T. Financial, 199
Cameron, Dr. Donald Ewen, 220
Celanese, 198
Center for Disease Control, 222, 250
Central Intelligence Agency, 219, 220
Chase Manhatten Bank, 195
Christian Identity, 67
Christianity, 66, 67, 69, 82, 115
Chrysler, 199
Cities Service, 198

City of London,, 167
Columbus, 132, 135, 136, 137
Company of the Bank of England, 143, 145
Conspiracy Theory of History, 18, 202
Continental Army, 150
Continental Congress, 148, 150, 157
Continental Oil, 199
Controllers, 61
Council on Foreign Relation, 87
Crimean War, 213
Cult of Isis, 17, 114, 121
Cumbey, Constance, 68
Czar of Russia, 18

D

Dark Gods, 47
Darwin, Charles, 34
David, Veidel, 174
Declaration of Independence, 142, 149, 157
Delta, 198
Depuis, 123
Douglass, Dr. William Campbell, 217, 223
Dow, 198
Dulles, Allan, 220
Dulles, John Foster, 100
DuPont, 198
Dwarfs, 45

E

Earl of Montgomery, 141
Earl of Northampton, 141
Earl of Pembroke, 140
Earl of Salisbury, 141
Eastern, 103, 145, 198
Easy Reader, 235
Egypt, 45, 76, 83, 213, 214
Egyptain War, 214
Elisah, 39

Energetics, 108
English, 29, 134, 142, 143, 144, 146, 152, 184, 186
ENLIL, 31, 32
Enoch, 25, 29, 39, 40
Epic of Creation, 33, 35
Eridu, 32
Eve, 31, 36, 37, 38
Exxon, 194, 196

F

Fairies, 45
Fama Fraternitatis, 118
Fay, Bernard, 116
Federal Reserve System, 145
First National City Bank (CitiCorp), 195
Fleming, Ian, 60
Food and Drug Administration, 239
Fort Detrick, Maryland, 218, 232
Franco-Prussian, 213
Frederick II, 153, 154, 173, 174
Freedom of Information Act, 239
Freemasonry, 115, 116, 117, 118, 124, 150, 153
Freeport Sulphur, 197
French Revolution, 79, 117, 159, 175, 202, 204, 205, 206, 207

G

Gabriel, 44
Gajdusek, Carlton, 233
Garden of Eden, 26, 28
Gorbachev, Michael, 97
Gordon, Dr. J. Nicholas, 226
Grand Lodge of England, 124
Grand Master of the Knights Templar, 206
Grand Orient Masonic Lodges of France, 203
Grant, Dr. Robert G., 222
Great Society, 98
Great War, 88

Greys, 48
Gulf, 198

H

Hall, Manley P., 65
Hambro Family, 181
Hambro, Carl Joachim, 181, 182
Hambros Bank, Ltd, 182, 183
Hamilton, William, 13
Haynau, 174
Heavenly Council, 29
Heimrod, 174
Herzl, Theodor, 79
Hessenstein, 174
Historical Office of the State Department, 100
Hoagland, Richard C., 45
Holloman Air Force Base, 49
Holy Grail, 120
Holy See, 205
House of Rothschild, 169, 177, 180, 188, 211
House, Colonel Edward Mandell, 88

I

IBM, 197
IGIGI, 37
Illuminati, 62, 73, 77, 78, 82, 155, 157, 158, 159, 203, 205
Imps, 45
Inland Steel, 197
International Basic Economy Corporation, 197
International Harvester, 197
International Paper, 197
Invisible College, 138
IT&T, 197

J

Jack the Ripper Murders, 122
Jacobin Clubs, 204
Jacques DeMolay, 206

James II, 123
Jesuits, 77, 155, 156
Jewish Cabala, 119
John Hancock, 150
Johnson, Lyndon Baines President, 98

K

Katzenback, Nicholas de B., 103
King George III, 149, 173
King Louis XVI, 202, 206
King Otto, 182
Kissinger, Henry, 86, 87
Knights of Christ, 135
Knights of the Temple, 133, 206
Knights Templar, 120, 123, 132, 133, 135, 144, 206, 207

L

Lagash, 32
Larak, 32
Larsa, 32
Lenin, Vladimir Ilych (Ulyanov), 99
Leonardo da Vinci, 136
Long Island Lighting, 197
Loranzo de Medici, 136
Lord Southampton, 140

M

MacArthur, Dr. Leonard, 253
Mackenzie, Kenneth, 126
Mackey, Albert G., 81
Madame Guillotine, 208
Magician, Cagliostro, 205
Maitreya, 68
Marathon Oil, 197
Marshall Soult, 79, 212
Martin, Henri, 82
Marx, Karl, 82
Mayor of the City, 167
Men-in-Black, 84
Merck, 198

Merovingian Dynasty, 121
Meyer Amschel, 172, 173, 174, 176, 177, 178, 179, 202
Michael, 44, 113, 118, 120, 121, 132, 135, 141, 207
Mills, Walter, 88
Minnesota Mining & Manufacturing, 197
Mirabeau, 158, 208
MJ-12, 58
Mobil, 195
Mobil Oil, 196
Monsanto, 198
Morocco "Affair, 215
Mutually Assured Destruction, 95

N

Napoleon, 156, 175, 211, 212
Napoleonic War, 213
Napoleonic Wars, 188, 211
National Airlines, 197
National Cancer Institute, 232
National Cash Register, 197
National Distillers, 198
National Institute of Health's Laboratory of Central Nervous System Studies, 233
National Steel, 197
Nectar of the Gods, 30
New Jerusalem, 136
New World Order, 65, 85, 117
Nippur, 32
Noble, Dr. G. Bernard, 100
Northwest Airlines, 197

O

Oak Island, 139
O'Brien, Christian, 25, 27, 41
Office of Strategic Services, 220
Old Cornish, 29
Old Irish, 29
Old Welsh, 29
Olin Mathison, 198

Omega Press, 3
Omni magazine, 233
Order of Illuminated Ones, 77
Order of the Helmet, 137
Order of the Temple, 135
Ossinsky, V. V., 105
Owen, Dr. Orville Ward, 139

P

Partition of Siam, 214
Paterson, William, 143, 144
Penn Central, 198
Persian Conflict, 215
Pfizer, 198
Philippe IV, 133
Pittsburgh Plate Glass, 198
Polio inoculation program, 239
Post 120 Annos Patebo, 119
Priest Kings, 72, 75, 76
Priest-Kings, 72
Prince Wilhelm of Denmark, 183
Prince William, 173, 174, 176
Proclamation of Rebellion, 149

Q

Quaker Oats, 197
Queen Anne's War, 152, 153

R

R.H. Macy, 199
Rappaport, Jon, 235
RED MENACE, 59
Rockefeller family, 191
Roosevelt, Franklin D., 18
Rosenkreutz, Christian, 118, 119
Rothschild Family, 149, 162, 163, 170, 171, 172, 175, 177, 179, 180, 182, 188, 212
Rousseau, 82, 153
Russian-Japanese, 214
Russian-Turkish, 213

S

S.S. Kresge, 199
Schmugner, Doctor W., 249
Secret societies, 47, 73
Serpent, 37
Shakespeare, William, 137, 138
Shell, 198
Shuruppak, 32
SIMIAN VIRUS 40, 242, 243
Sippar, 32
<u>Sitchin, Zecharia</u>, 24, 26
Snead, Dr. Eva Lee, 238
Son Tay, 42
Sons of God, 39
Sons of the Light, 43
Spanish American, 214
Sperry Rand, 197
Standard of CA, 196
Standard of California, 195, 197
Standard Oil, 193, 194
Standard Oil Trust, 194
State Department, 60, 62, 92, 100, 101, 102, 104
Stauffer Chemical, 198
Sudan War, 214
Sutton, Antony C., 97
SV-40, 241, 242, 243, 244, 252

T

Talleyrand, 211
Temple of Solomon, 122, 141
Tesla, Nikola, 107
Texaco, 197
Texas
    El Paso, 3, 4, 5
The Insiders, 73
The Lost Realms, 24, 48
The Order of the Rosy Cross, 115, 118, 120, 121
The Prieure de Sion, 115
Tower of Babel, 51
Tree of Knowledge, 31
Trolls, 45

Tropical Disease Center, 228
Turkish War, 213
TWA, 198

U

U.F.O.s, 53, 125
Underground City, 13
Unidentified Flying Objects, 5, 9, 16, 57, 71
Union Carbide, 199
Union Oil, 198
United Airlines, 197

V

Van der Notten, 174
Virginia Company, 140

W

Walter Reed Army Medical Center, 247
Wang. Connie, 4
War of Spanish Succession, 152, 153
War of the Immortals, 49
Washington, George, 78, 150, 151, 153, 154
Watchers, 37, 38, 39, 40, 41, 42, 43, 44, 45, 47, 52
Weishaupt, Adam, 77, 78
Westinghouse, 197
Wheeling-Pittsburgh Steel, 197
William III, 143
Wilson, Woodrow President, 87, 88, 102, 129
World Health Organization., 218, 223, 247
World War I, 215
Wright, Pearce, 247

X

Xerox, 197

www.ingramcontent.com/pod-product-compliance
Lightning Source LLC
Chambersburg PA
CBHW030312080526
44584CB00012B/538